CITY OF LONDON
PAST

First published 1995
by Historical Publications Ltd
32 Ellington Street, London N7 8PL
(Tel: 0171-607 1628)

© **Richard Tames 1995**

ISBN 0 948667 31 1
British Library Cataloguing-in-Publication Data
A catalogue record for this book is available from the British Library.

Typeset in Palatino by Historical Publications Ltd
Reproduction by G & J Graphics, London EC1
Printed in Zaragoza, Spain by Edelvives.

The illustrations used in this book were provided by the Author and Historical Publications Ltd.

CITY OF LONDON
PAST

Richard Tames

HISTORICAL PUBLICATIONS

1. A quiet enclave in the City in the 1920s. The artist is sketching in Huggin Lane off Upper Thames Street.

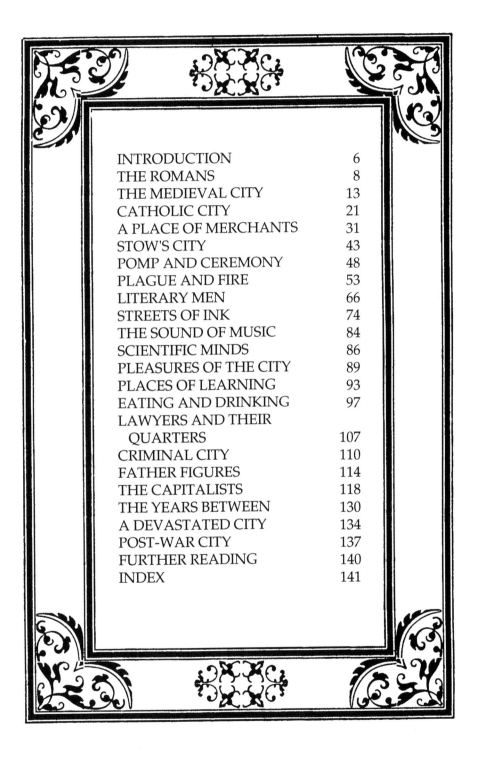

Introduction to a Hidden City

The City is where commuters work during the week and visitors wander at weekends through deserted streets, seeking to summon up the sights and sounds and spirits of those who departed decades, rather than the day, before. For those with time to pause, remember or imagine there is still so much to see or summon up. Some of the City's architecture is still world-class. Many of its ghosts certainly are. A forcing-house of ambition, the City has also been a magnet for talent throughout the twenty centuries of its existence. Chaucer, Milton, Gray and Keats were all born in the City. Wesley, Thackeray, Coleridge and Lamb were all educated in the City. Holbein, Shakespeare, Van Dyck and Johnson were drawn to live in the City. It was in the City that Harvey discovered the circulation of the blood. It was in the City that commercial publishing and newspapers were truly born. The City was the birthplace of the Bank of England, the insurance business and the modern news agency. It was in the City that plans were laid and finance raised to colonise the New World. It was the City and not just Venice which "held the gorgeous East in fee".

The City has always been a place where people worked. That was and is and doubtless always will be its *raison d'être*. But the City, whose chief product is now money in a hundred different forms, was once a place where almost anything could be bought and many things were actually made – by people who actually lived there. Cheapside, famed for its goldsmiths and jewellers in Tudor times, was still the capital's main shopping street a hundred and fifty years ago. With a population of around 130,000, the City at that time was still the most populous part of the metropolis. The father of the poet William Morris could still commute by stage-coach from leafy Walthamstow but most people who did not live at their place of employment walked to it. Even the Rothschilds still literally lived 'over the shop'. Over the next half century that traditional pattern of City life began to change decisively with the coming of the railways. Domestic dwellings extended or part-converted to accommodate counting-houses and workshops gave way to purpose-built blocks of offices with no accommodation for residents, other than, perhaps, a caretaker. The City ceased to be the most densely populated residential area and lost population in absolute and not just relative terms. By the beginning of the present century it had fallen to 27,000. Nowadays it is less than a fifth of that number.

Over thirty years ago the writer Naomi Lewis pursued the hidden past buried beneath Liverpool Street station, uncovering successively a meadow, a monastery, a mad-house and a music-hall. She concluded that the City was "where every street and lane and spire leads straight into history.... where you find more by being lost than in any part of England." You still can – even if now you have to make the eyes of your imagination strain that much harder.

The City is literally layered with its history. An area scarcely more than a couple of acres in extent, and currently occupied by a single building, will suffice to demonstrate the point. The main entrance to this building straddles what was once the line of a garden path, leading to a medieval manor house, which was the home of Italian bankers and later of Henry V's personal surgeon. Elizabeth Fry, Quaker prison reformer, spent the first nine years of her married life in a house on this site. The poet Thomas Hood was born there in another one. The black magician attached to James I's unpopular favourite, the Duke of Buckingham, died there, after being pelted insensible by a Cheapside mob. So did Thomas Tusser, failed farmer and composer of the doggerel *Five Hundred Points of Good Husbandrie*. A Roman millstone has been found there – and the bones of plague victims. A church stood there for over six centuries, in three incarnations, the last designed by Wren. There has also been a chantry chapel, a Congregational church, a Rose Tavern and a prison where the inmates were fed on scraps from the Lord Mayor's table and the last slave in England was kept confined. Butchers scalded hogs there. Lyons' 'nippies' served teas there. In 1259 a bootmaker was in business there, in the 1920s a branch of Manfield's shoe-stores. A furrier and a haberdasher, a linen-draper, a brewer and a tobacconist, printers and booksellers have all done business there. Nowadays this site in Poultry, at the eastern end of Cheapside, is covered by the headquarters of the Midland Bank, the last great project of Sir Edwin Lutyens, designer of the Cenotaph. So much history in such a little space, the story of the City itself in miniature. What follows in this book must, therefore, omit a hundred times more than it can include.

Swept by fire a dozen times before the holocausts of 1666 and 1940, devasted piecemeal by developers in this century, as in the past, the City has proved itself a city capable of rebirth in many different forms but one that will not – cannot – die. Like Wren's mighty St Paul's, hemmed in by modern mediocrity, the City sometimes seems in danger of being overwhelmed by enormities of its own creation. Somehow, so far, it has defiantly lived up to the terse motto Wren had inscribed beneath the phoenix which surmounts the south transept of his masterpiece – RESURGAM – "I will rise again".

2. 'A view of part of the antient remains of London Wall now standing near Postern Row, Tower Hill in the parish of All Hallows Barking; September 1818.

ANTIENT REMAINS of LONDON WALL,

Tower Hill in the Parish of

SEPTEMBER 1818.

Robert Wilkinson, *N.º 125 Fenchurch Street.*

The Romans

Rome claimed a precise date for its own foundation – but not for that of its creation, London. The first bridge over the Thames was built *c*.AD50, some yards downstream from the present line of London Bridge, taking advantage of gravel deposits on either bank to give it a firm footing. Previously unsettled, the site had several attractions for the conqueror – slightly elevated and well-drained in a low-lying region, with soil suitable for brickmaking, fresh water from the rivers Fleet and Walbrook and a tidal river capable of providing anchorage for large ships. Politically, it had the advantage of lying at the junction of a number of tribal territories.

RAZED AND REBUILT

The inexorable annexation of the island was brutally checked in AD60 by the revolt of a Norfolk tribe, the Iceni. Led by their formidable Queen, Boudicca, they burned undefended Londinium and massacred those of its inhabitants who had not fled with its garrison. The city was, however, quickly rebuilt and prospered under the administration of Gaius Julius Alpinus Classicianus, the Roman procurator, who shrewdly decided to handle the aftermath of revolt by promoting the province's commerce rather than punishing its people. Under Agricola, father-in-law of the historian Tacitus, this policy was continued. A timber quay and stone warehouses were built along the river front on reclaimed land and the local population was introduced to the pleasures of the Roman bath at a new establishment built at Huggin Hill in Upper Thames Street. A smaller one, probably for the use of the military rather than the general public, was later built at Cheapside.

The nucleus of reborn London was around Cornhill, the highest point immediately to the north of the bridge. Where Leadenhall market now stands was the site of the basilica, a combination of town hall and law court; at 164 yards it was longer than any other north of the Alps and faced onto a forum far larger than today's Trafalgar Square. The governor's palace, a rambling complex covering 13,000 square metres, overlooked the river from a site now covered by Cannon Street station. Primarily a commercial and governmental rather than military centre, London did not acquire walls until *c*.AD200. The city's twelve-acre fort was incorporated into the circuit of the walls at their north-west corner, where the Museum of London now stands. It was not a major citadel but rather a transit camp for troops beginning and ending tours of duty and a base for the modest garrison which performed ceremonial and security duties in the capital. Another major facility was the amphi-

3. *Standing guard by the enigmatically-named London Stone. This piece of shaped Clipsham stone was, at the time of this photograph in 1926, set into the wall of St Swithin's church in Cannon Street, but is now similarly inserted into the building occupied by the Overseas Chinese Banking Corporation in the same street. One suggestion is that it was part of the perimeter wall of the Roman governor's palace which occupied the site of Cannon Street station.*

theatre, undiscovered until 1988, which covered what is now Guildhall Yard.

By AD122 London was important enough to merit a visit from the restless Hadrian, who would have been greeted by a cosmopolitan citizenry composed not only of Romanised Britons and a few senior appointees from Italy itself, but also a substantial proportion from neighbouring Gaul and the Rhineland, a sprinkling of merchants from the ports of the Mediterranean and an honour guard which might have included men recruited as far away as North Africa.

DEFENCE AND RELIGION

A few years after the emperor's visit fire destroyed about a hundred acres of the city centre, a severe blow from which it took some decades to recover. The construction of circuit walls around the end of the second century was probably prompted by the political turmoil of the day. Almost three metres thick and over six high, built of Kentish ragstone with a supporting bank of earth inside and a V-shaped ditch outside, they enclosed some 330 acres, making Londinium not only the largest city in the Roman province of Britannia but also the fifth largest of the western half of the empire. The walls were further strengthened by external bastions on the eastern side as the security situation deteriorated in the late fourth century. They were still performing their defensive role over a thousand years later; their last refurbishment came in 1476, when brick battlements were added to them.

As was customary, burials took place outside the walls, in cemeteries either side of the approach roads to Newgate and Bishopsgate and on the south side of the road to Aldgate.

The religious life of Londinium was typical of the empire in its eclecticism. There was certainly a temple to the emperor, whose worship was a state cult; but, beyond requiring formal acceptance of this requirement, Roman policy was to tolerate additional allegiances as a matter of private preference. The figure of a hunter god displayed in Southwark cathedral may have come from the domestic altar of a villa which once stood there, implying the acceptance of purely local deities. The less densely settled area west of the Walbrook was probably a religious precinct, including possibly a shrine to the Egyptian goddess, Isis, and another to Diana on the high ground where St Paul's now stands. But this is speculative. What is certain is the location of the temple of Mithras, whose cult, originating in Persia, appealed particularly to

4. A plan of the main features of Roman London so far discovered. The Forum and basilica are on the site of today's Leadenhall Market, and the fort is now occupied by the Museum of London and adjoining buildings. The amphitheatre, on the site of Guildhall Yard, was discovered in 1988 during the construction of the Guildhall Art Gallery.

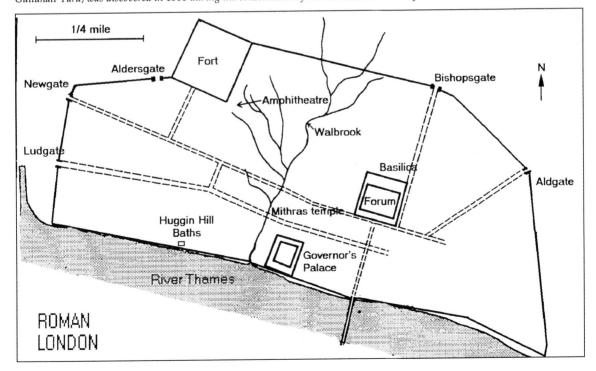

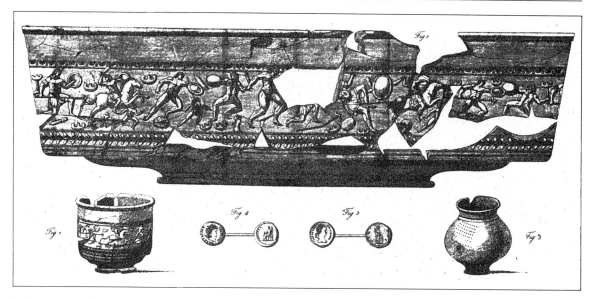

5. Roman antiquities found in London in 1786. From Archæologia, *vol. viii.*

the peripatetic traders, troops and officials who constituted a significant proportion of the local population. It was discovered in 1954 when the foundations
were being dug for Bucklersbury House and was
relocated about a hundred metres to the west in its
present prominent position on Queen Victoria Street.

Tradition attributes the foundation of a Christian
church, where St Michael's, Cornhill now stands, to a
shadowy King Lucius around AD170. What is certain
is that Londinium was represented by its Bishop,
Restitutus, at a council held in Arles, southern France,
in 314. Fear of Christian persecution probably moti-
vated the burial of the Mithraic altar which was found
beneath the floor of the temple.

LONDINIUM LOST – AND FOUND
Roman rule in Britain effectively ended in 410 when
its people were informed by the beleaguered emperor
Honorius that they must shift for their own defences.
It was recorded that in 457 a beaten Romano-British
force took shelter within the city walls. After that the
historical record is blank for a century and a half.

Londinium lies some twelve to twenty feet beneath
the modern streets of the City. Well-grounded knowledge of its layout and life was a by-product of the
rebuilding which followed the Great Fire of 1666 and
of the construction of modern sewers and the Underground from mid-Victorian times onwards. In two
locations near Tower Hill large fragments of the tomb
of Classicianus himself were recovered. The magnificent polychrome Bucklersbury mosaic was unearthed
in 1869 during the making of Queen Victoria Street.

*6. Bacchus on a tiger is depicted in this mosaic unearthed in
Leadenhall Street in 1803.*

The construction of contemporary high-rise buildings, requiring deep foundations, invariably throws
further light on Londinium's past. Only in 1988 did
the construction of a new art gallery next to the
Guildhall reveal the hitherto unknown location of
Londinium's amphitheatre.

The Medieval City

As a farming people the Saxons had little taste for city life and were hesitant to occupy deserted Londinium, preferring to found settlements well outside its walls at such places as Stepney or Bermondsey. The tribe known as Berecingas established themselves well to the east in an area which took their name to become Barking, just as the Gillingas to the west gave their name to Ealing.

LUNDENWIC

A passing reference in a royal charter of the 670s to the 'port of London where ships land' clearly implies the continuing importance of commerce but excavations over the course of the last decade suggests that the 'port' of 'Lundenwic' was located further upstream, on the bend of the river along the Strand, between Aldwych and Charing Cross. St Paul's stood within the City walls, as did All Hallows (by the not yet built Tower) and there may also have been a wooden royal palace, possibly in the Wood Street area, where there was a church dedicated to St Alban.

LUNDENBERG

Massive Viking raids decimated London's exposed population in 842 and 851. In 871-2 the raiders made London their winter base. Alfred of Wessex forced them out over the following decade and formally re-established the occupation of the walled city – Lundenberg – in 886, allowing unprotected upstream Lundenwic to revert to fields. Lundenberg was the crucial anchor for the line of fortified burghs which protected the frontier between Saxon and Dane and marked its eastern extremity, the agreed boundary lying just a few miles away – the River Lea, which was later to mark off London from Essex. The southern end of London Bridge was also fortified to become 'the south werk' – Southwark.

The Saxons overlaid much of the Roman street pattern with their own, which has substantially survived to the present. The long curves of Lombard Street and Fenchurch Street probably originated as through-routes between ruins, such as the former basilica. Down by the river a new grid-plan was imposed. The area north of West Cheap (Cheapside) was reoccupied. Little, beyond repairing the walls, was attempted in the way of ambitious building. Perhaps the crumbling banked seats of the ancient

7. The gates of medieval London. Aldgate, Bishopsgate, Aldersgate, Newgate and Ludgate were part of the Roman wall around the the City, while Cripplegate was originally a gate leading from the Roman fort; Moorgate was a later postern gate into the Moor fields. Bridge Gate was on London Bridge. All the Wall gates were demolished in the 1760s

amphitheatre were used for meetings of the folkmoot. The 'old stone building' referred to in a document of 889 was probably the Roman bath-house, disused for centuries, but still standing, its purpose incomprehensible to the city's new residents. A landing-place for cargo was carved out of the river front nearby this ancient survivor at what is now Queenhithe but was originally Etheldredshythe, named after Alfred's son-in-law, the Ealdorman of Mercia, who supervised the reoccupation of the city. Billingsgate was also established as a landing and loading point and a market for produce.

The title of 'Ealdorman' born by the City's governor was also given to the chief citizen of each of the twenty-odd wards into which it was divided for administrative purposes. In time of peace the aldermen adjudicated in disputes and in time of war acted as commanders of their able-bodied neighbours.

By the reign of Athelstan (925-39) London's commercial importance is attested by the fact that it was authorised to have more coiners than any other town. Another sign of its wealth was the high quality of jewellery produced there. Although royal councils often met in London, they could meet elsewhere and London was not to be regarded as the capital of the whole country until the following century.

In 994 London successfully resisted another massive Viking onslaught but in 1016 the country was obliged to accept Danish rule under Knut. After his death the throne reverted to the Saxon Edward, whose piety impelled him to commence the building of a great new abbey and adjacent palace upstream at Westminster, thus creating a second nucleus for London's growth, a royal rival to the commercial City. The tension between these two centres of power, the one primarily political, the other primarily economic, would shape the entire succeeding history, not only of the future metropolis, but of the nation itself.

THE NORMANS AND AFTER

"William, King, greets William, Bishop, and Godfrey, Portreeve, and all the burghers within London, French and English, friendlike. And I will that both be worthy of all the rights of which ye both were worthy in King Edward's day. And I will that every child be

8. Baynard's Castle, built by a follower of William the Conqueror to defend the western side of the City. The castle was rebuilt at least twice and survived until the Great Fire when all but one turret (itself demolished in 1720) was destroyed.

his father's heir after his father's day. And I will not suffer that any man offer you wrong."

Thus William, Duke of Normandy, having burned Southwark as a hint, sealed a surly bargain with the City, rather than attempt to take it by storm. Twenty years later the City was omitted from the great inquisition which compiled the Domesday book, but, as a reminder of sovereign power, in 1078 William commenced building the Tower of London at the eastern edge of the City. At its then western edge, the king's vassal, Ralph Baynard, threw up Baynard's Castle and immediately to the north of that stood short-lived Mountfichet, a moated keep, dominating Ludgate.

The Tower both protected the City from marauders and menaced the City's population. Since then it has remained a symbol of state security, guarding at different times the person of the monarch, traitors, archives, an arsenal, a menagerie of savage beasts, the royal mint and the Crown jewels.

Professor Roy Porter has observed that Westminster developed as a Versailles to London's Paris – "monarch and municipality were at arm's length." And that was how the Londoners liked it. In the twelfth century they gained the right to collect their own taxes and choose sheriffs, who acted as representatives of royal authority in each county.

At a time when monarchs relied on feudal levies and mercenaries to provide the ultimate sanction behind their rule, London's citizen militia could prove decisive. When Stephen and Matilda duelled for the succession to Henry I's throne, Londoners, backing Stephen, drove Matilda's forces from the City. Under John the City sided with the barons to extort the Magna Carta. Under Henry III it resisted the restoration of direct royal authority within its walls.

In 1381 the imposition of an undiscriminating poll tax provoked the men of Essex and Kent into general revolt. Whether through sympathy or fear the ordinary citizens of London opened their gates to the rebellious peasantry. The Archbishop of Canterbury and the hated Treasurer of the kingdom were hauled from their hiding-place in the Tower and summarily despatched at Tower Hill. Only by a mixture of cajolery and lies did the boy king Richard II and his startled courtiers and captains buy time while they regrouped their forces for a decisive counterstroke. The rebels were then hunted down and hanged, or worse – but there were no more poll-taxes.

9. Norman London, as depicted in Sir Walter Besant's Early London. *The earliest religious houses to settle in London are shown. The Dominican (Black) friars were granted the site of Baynard's Castle at the end of the 13th century and the London Wall was realigned westwards to include their grounds.*

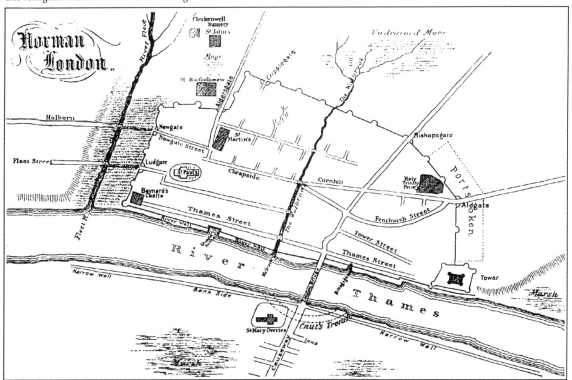

10. *Possibly the earliest painting of London. It was made by an unknown artist in the reign of Henry VII to illustrate a book of poems compiled by Charles, Duc d'Orleans, during his imprisonment in the Tower of London after the battle of Agincourt. The Duke is seen in the White Tower of the Tower of London writing home, and is also shown looking out of an upper window and depicted riding home after his ransom had been paid. The arcaded building behind the Tower is Billingsgate market, and behind that is London Bridge.*

11. *The killing of Wat Tyler, leader of the Peasants' Revolt, by William Walworth, Lord Mayor of London. Tyler was actually stabbed, rather than decapitated, as this later illustration suggests*

12. *The medieval gabled architecture of London is suggested in this 17th-century print depicting the procession of Charles I's mother-in-law, Marie de Medici, through Cheapside.*

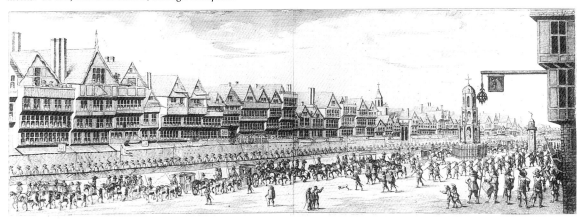

LONDON BRIDGE

Until 1750 London had only one bridge across the Thames and it was reckoned to be one of the wonders of Europe. The Romans built the first, wooden bridge and it was rebuilt several times over the following thousand years, most notably after 1014, when King Ethelred and King Olaf of Norway burned and pulled it down to frustrate a besieging Danish army. A gale swept it away again in 1091 and a fire in 1136. The first stone bridge, standing on nineteen arches, was constructed between 1176 and 1209 under the direction of Peter, Chaplain of St Mary Colechurch, Cheapside, who was buried in a chapel on the bridge, dedicated to Thomas Becket. The finished work is said to have been 900 feet long, twenty broad and about thirty feet above water-level at low tide. Even before the bridge was completed houses were being built on it. Later dwellings were up to seven storeys high. A rental of 1358 reveals that there were no less than 138 shops on it, making it a veritable medieval Oxford Street. During the reign of Elizabeth I two notable additions were made to the bridge. Nonsuch House, a splendid prefabricated wooden residence was brought over from Holland in 1579 and assembled using only pegs, not nails. In 1582 Peter Moritz, a Dutchman, installed mills beneath two of the arches to provide subscribers with a pumped water supply.

At the Southwark end of London bridge was a drawbridge and a gatehouse upon which the heads of traitors were displayed from 1305, when the head of Scottish patriot William Wallace was put there, until 1678. The heads of Sir Thomas More and Thomas Cromwell featured there and a German visitor in the 1590s counted over thirty. The heads were parboiled in the gatehouse before being tarred, to discourage scavenging birds from stripping them of their features. Wat Tyler took the bridge without a fight after threatening to burn it down during the Peasants' Revolt of 1381 and Jack Cade did the same in 1450 – though his head eventually ended up on the gatehouse roof. Henry V crossed it in triumph after his victory at Agincourt in 1415, as did Charles II at his restoration to the throne in 1660.

A fire damaged the bridge severely in 1212 and again in 1633 but some two thirds was spared by the Great Fire of 1666. Between 1758 and 1762 the houses were at last removed and two central arches replaced by a single one to enable larger ships to pass through. The Southwark gateway was demolished in 1760. The Royal Arms which once adorned it can now be seen on the King's Arms Tavern in Newcomen Street, off Borough High Street.

Between 1823 and 1831 a new, granite bridge was built up-stream of the old one to the designs of Rennie and King William Street was driven through existing

13. *Peter Visscher's view of London Bridge, from the south-west showing the medieval and Tudor buildings along its length. A grisly array of traitors' heads may be seen on the gatehouse on the Southwark side. Notice the pilings around the piers which greatly narrowed the space between them and made the bridge a virtual weir when the ebb tide ran high. To the west of Southwark cathedral (then the church of St Mary Overie) at the southern end of the bridge can be seen the riverside palace of the Bishop of Winchester. To the north the skyline of the City is dominated by the spires of its many parish churches.*

buildings to link it with Bank junction. It is this second stone London Bridge which was demolished and reconstructed at Lake Havasu City in Arizona, with the exception of a single, surviving arch which still bears the roadway at the southern end of the present bridge, built between 1967 and 1972.

14. *The chapel on London Bridge dedicated to St Thomas Becket. A reconstruction by Gordon Home, based on an illuminated manuscript in the British Museum and published in his book* Old London Bridge *(1931).*

15. *London Bridge from the west, by Samuel Scott c.1750.*

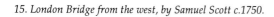

Catholic City

Despite the survival of such street names as Ave Maria Lane and Paternoster Square, the City's Christian credentials rest on initially shaky foundations. Although tradition holds that St Paul's was founded within a decade of St Augustine's arrival in Kent in 597, the faith does not appear to have established itself firmly in London for another half century, thanks largely, it seems, to the inhabitants' attachment to trade with the pagan Frisians. By default, therefore, Canterbury assumed the primacy of the church in England, although London had originally been intended for that honour by the Papacy.

SAINTS AND CULTS

The dominant figure in the early history of Christianity in London is St Erkenwald, (d.693), Bishop of London. Certainly rich, and possibly royal, he founded religious houses at Chertsey and Barking, the latter of which was headed by his sister, Ethelburga. Erkenwald died at Barking, which subsequently became the second largest monastery in England and served as the residence of William I in the immediate aftermath of the Norman conquest. Erkenwald is also credited with the building of Bishopsgate and the first stone St Paul's. His shrine in the cathedral, embellished to magnificence over the centuries, became a major object of veneration and pilgrimage.

The reforming St Dunstan (909-88), reviver of English monasticism and deviser of the Coronation service, after a roller-coaster career of royal favour punctuated by exile, became Bishop of London in 959 and Archbishop of Canterbury the following year. His alleged skill as a metalworker made him the patron of the City's locksmiths, goldsmiths and jewellers.

In the eyes of medieval Londoners both these venerable figures were to be overshadowed by the cult of Thomas Becket (1118-70). Born in Cheapside at its junction with Ironmonger Lane, he was the son of a wealthy mercer and was customarily known as Thomas of London. Shining as an administrator, diplomat and soldier, he served as Constable of the Tower, Chancellor of England and Archbishop of Canterbury before quarrelling with Henry II over the rights of the Church and embracing a martyr's death. He was revered as far away as Iceland, Sicily and Armenia and most of all in the city of his birth; of the numerous pilgrim souvenir badges excavated in London, no less than a quarter depict him. Londoners honoured him by founding the Hospital of St Thomas of the Military Order of Acre on the site of the house in which he had been born. The chapel on newly-completed London Bridge was also dedicated to his memory. And, as St Thomas, Becket henceforth ap-

16. *Thomas Becket, a fifteenth-century representation.*

peared beside St Paul, the City's patron saint, on the official seal of the Corporation.

PARISHES

The first extensive written description of London occurs in the preface to the biography of Becket written around 1180 by the monk William FitzStephen. It is a paean of virtually unstinting praise, recording every metropolitan delight from skating on the frozen marsh at Moorfields in the winter to guzzling piping-hot fast-food down by the river. The only shortcomings of London life that the author was willing to concede were the frequency of fires (there were seven major ones between 1077 and 1135) and "the immoderate drinking of fools". A special point of pride was the more than one hundred parish churches crammed within the City walls and spilling over into the surrounding suburbs.

Most parishes covered no more than a few acres. Along the riverside between Blackfriars and London Bridge, where the population was at its densest, over a score of churches were packed in. They functioned as both spiritual and secular centres for parishioners, representing both a focus for communal celebrations and the lowest tier of local government. Their dedications reveal both a resilient pride in local traditions and an openness to cosmopolitan influences. Christopher is usually thought of as the patron of travellers, but the City had four churches named for Botolph, his Saxon equivalent. St Alban's, Wood Street, commemorated the first English martyr, St Alfege, London Wall an Archbishop of Canterbury brutally bludgeoned to death by Danes in 1012 for gallantly refusing to be ransomed. But alongside such obviously English saints as Swithin, Mildred and Dunstan, there were also dedications to the French saints Martin, Giles, Dionis (Denis) and Vedast and the Scandinavians, Magnus and Olave (Olaf).

RELIGIOUS HOUSES

The later Middle Ages witnessed the building of over a dozen major religious houses, proud precincts of privilege, mostly located around the fringes of the City walls, where the air was sweeter and there was room for gardens, orchards and shaded walks. The foundation of St Martin's le Grand by Ingelric, a Saxon courtier of the Confessor, was confirmed in 1068 by the Conqueror; it became famous as Eng-

17. (Below) Great St Helen's

18. (Right) St Katharine Cree, Leadenhall Street, rebuilt in 1628-30. Its name is thought to be a corruption of Christchurch.

19. The Charterhouse buildings in the eighteenth century. Founded as a Carthusian monastery in 1370, the buildings were used from 1611 for a school for 44 poor boys and a hospital for 80 poor gentlemen, begun by Thomas Sutton.

land's largest and safest sanctuary for thieves and debtors, only traitors and Jews being turned away. The fact that the Prior of Holy Trinity at Aldgate served as Alderman of Portsoken Ward shows how closely church and state were intertwined. But the relationship between sacred and secular was not always harmonious. The Priory built the church of St Katharine Cree within its precincts to re-establish its separation from parishioners who had previously used the priory church. The Augustinian nuns of St Helen's, Bishopsgate did worship in the parish church – but in a separate, sectioned-off nave of their own. The wealth of the City's inhabitants fuelled their piety. St Helen's was founded by the son of a goldsmith, Charterhouse by one of Edward III's most gallant knights, who had already donated a burial ground for victims of the Black Death.

Towering over all other religious establishments, quite literally, was Old St Paul's, the fourth incarnation of the cathedral, begun after the burning of the third in 1087 and completed in 1327. Its spire was the tallest ever built, its two bell towers so large they were used as prisons, its rose window so glorious that it was routinely imitated by embroiderers. The outdoor pulpit known as Paul's Cross was used for both high-profile preaching and penances; Carlyle called it *"The Times* newspaper of the Middle Ages".

20. Paul's Cross in the seventeenth century. Public announcements such as Papal Bulls or royal proclamations were made from Paul's Cross and sermons were also preached here. The Cross, on the north-east side of the churchyard, was a wooden pulpit surmounted by a conical lead roof. It was taken down in 1643 and a memorial now marks the site.

THE FRIARS

The high walls surrounding religious houses and St Paul's symbolized, as well as protected, their aloofness from the mundane lives of the citizens. The friars, by contrast, came to preach the gospel on the streets and involve themselves in what would now be called programmes of social action among the poor. The first to arrive, the Franciscans or Greyfriars, settled themselves modestly in the shadow of the City abbatoirs, between St Paul's and Smithfield. The Dominicans (Blackfriars) eventually took over the site of the redundant fortifications at Baynard's Castle. Their headquarters became sufficiently important to host meetings of Parliament, the Court of Chancery and the Privy Council. The Carmelites (Whitefriars), a mendicant order, were established in Bouverie Street. Despite their proximity to the temptations of the metropolis they maintained their commitment to poverty and with it the respect of the people. During the Peasants' Revolt of 1381 they remained quite unmolested, when the nearby Savoy Palace, residence of the hated John of Gaunt, was sacked and fired. At the eastern end of the City were the Augustinian ('Austin') Friars and the Friars of the Cross ('Crutched Friars'). The Austins were likewise spared but respect for their sanctity had its limits; thirteen luckless Flemings who had taken refuge under their protection were dragged out and beheaded.

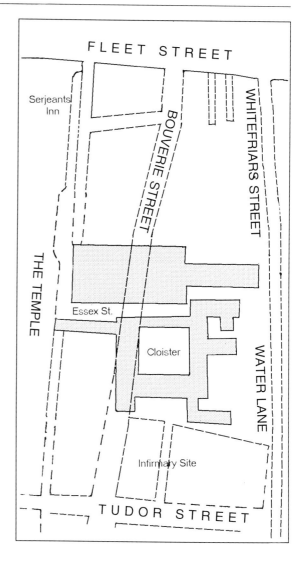

21. (Below) The remains of Blackfriars monastery, unearthed in 1872. From a painting by R. Rushen. The monastery was built to the far south-west of the City, overlooking the river Fleet as it disgorged into the Thames, with the City Wall diverted around it.

22. (Right) The site of the Whitefriars monastery between Fleet Street and the river. The buildings and precincts fell into disrepair after the Dissolution and later became the notoriously criminal area called Alsatia.

HOSPITALS

Religious hospitals also skirted the City on the east and north, combining the functions of hospice, hostel and retirement home as well as hospital in the modern sense. St Katharine's by the Tower enjoyed the personal patronage of successive queens of England, enabling it to survive the Dissolution in the 1530s. 'St Mary Spital' and the Bethlehem hospital both stood on Bishopsgate, the latter coming to specialise in the care of the 'distracted', a function so essential that, after the Dissolution, the City itself re-established Bethlehem ('Bedlam') as an asylum, first of all in Bridewell and, after 1675, in a handsome building at Moorfields, designed by City Surveyor Robert Hooke. Elsing Spital, named for its first prior, and more properly 'The Priory Hospital of St Mary's Within Cripplegate', was a retreat for the blind, housed in a former nunnery. St Bartholomew's Hospital, founded by the courtier Rahere at Smithfield in 1123, was not only the oldest of them all but destined to survive for almost nine centuries, becoming an outstanding centre of medical practice.

DISILLUSION AND DISSOLUTION

Far less regarded than the hospitals were the chantries, which began to proliferate during the fourteenth century, when the Church began vigorously to promote the doctrine of purgatory, encouraging the wealthy and fearful to endow chapels where appointed priests could chant masses for the spiritual relief of their patrons. Dick Whittington, a generous donor to such entirely worldly causes as a discreet maternity ward for unmarried mothers, bequeathed money to found a college of priests (hence College Hill) and an almshouse to perpetuate his memory and ease the affliction of his soul. As the wealthiest city in

23. The Hospital of St Bethlehem (Bedlam) was founded as a priory in 1247 in that part of Bishopsgate outside the City Wall. The first record of 'distracted' patients being treated here is in 1377. It was managed by the City after the Dissolution and removed to new buildings (shown below) on Moorfields in 1676. From the 17th century viewing the antics of the inmates was one of the diversions of Londoners – by then 'Bethlehem' had become corrupted to Bedlam, a word which entered the English language signifying scenes of uproar.

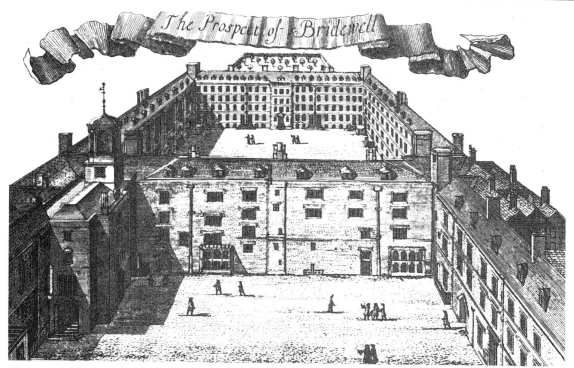

24. *Bridewell Hospital, between Fleet Street and the Thames, west of today's New Bridge Street; a print published in 1755. Built as a palace by Henry VIII, it was given to the City by Edward VI in 1553 for use as a secure place for vagrants and orphaned children. It later became a workhouse and prison. Mostly destroyed in the Great Fire, it was rebuilt and continued as a prison until 1855.*

the kingdom London had scores of chantries and thus hundreds of chantry priests, whose perfunctory duties got them generally regarded as idle parasites by many of those who did not benefit from their nominal interventions with the divine. This may have been a factor encouraging Londoners to give an attentive ear to the revolutionary Kentish 'hedge-priest' John Ball at the time of the Peasants' Revolt and to interest themselves in the subversive teachings of John Wyclif, first translator of the Bible into English. Wyclif's heresies were condemned by the Archbishop of Canterbury at a special council convened at Blackfriars the year after the crushing of the Peasants' Revolt. When an earthquake interrupted their proceedings those attending were no doubt shaken in more senses than one.

Despite the public immolation of Wyclif's followers, the Lollards, cells of clandestine Lollardy may have persisted in late medieval London. At the same time the standing of the local religious continued to decline in the eyes of the public. Chaucer's monk is portrayed as a fanatical huntsman, his friar as a seducer of City wives and his prioress, who "spake the frensshe of Stratforde-Atte-Bowe", as a simpering snob. Ecclesiastical officials, such as the Sum-

moner and Pardoner, are even less flatteringly portrayed. St Martin's le Grand became so notorious for the production of counterfeit jewellery that, in 1447, the Goldsmiths' Company was authorised to search for and seize all they could find. The nuns of St Helen's were reproved for their dancing, their pets and their ostentatious costumes. St Mary Spital and Holy Trinity both so mismanaged their finances as to fall deeply into debt.

Given this background, it becomes less surprising that the dissolution of the religious houses by Henry VIII met with so little popular resistance. Most of their clergy acquiesced in their fate. Only Charterhouse proved contumacious and paid a grisly price. Prior Houghton's invitation to discuss the King's supremacy got him, along with two of his fellows, hanged, drawn and quartered at Tyburn. Four more later suffered the same fate. Nine others were chained upright in Newgate until they starved to death.

Ten monastic chapels became parish churches but most monastic buildings were either converted to secular uses or demolished for their masonry, timbers and lead.

Austin Friars became a wine store before being handed over to the refugee Protestant Dutch congre-

25. *Carthusian monks being drawn on a hurdle to their execution. This bizarre print, from the British Museum, was published in Sir Walter Besant's* London in the Time of the Tudors *(1904).*

gation, in whose hands it has remained ever since. Greyfriars was used to store herrings until Edward VI founded Christ's Hospital school on its site. The Carmelites' house was divided up between the King's armourer and his physician, while its Great Hall was occasionally used as a playhouse. The priory of the Crutched Friars vanished entirely, its stone being used to repair the Tower and its land built over. The Leathersellers' Company acquired the dormitory of St Heien's. Charterhouse served as an aristocratic residence until 1611, when Thomas Sutton, bought it to turn it into a school for 44 poor boys and a hospital for 80 poor men. St Etheldreda's, the private chapel attached to the London residence of the Bishop of Ely, however, miraculously survived even the eighteenth century demolition of the episcopal residence itself and finally reverted to Roman Catholic hands in 1874.

By 1551 the Venetian ambassador could record with distaste that the whole City was "disfigured by the ruins of a multitude of churches and monasteries" but this apparent desolation proved but temporary. By releasing a third of the land in cramped London for redevelopment the Dissolution inaugurated a building boom without which the phenomenal population growth of Elizabeth's reign could never have been accommodated.

SURVIVORS OF THE FLAMES

Of the City's 'pre-Fire' churches only a handful survive.

All Hallows-by-the-Tower is a Saxon foundation of the seventh century, associated with Erkenwald's great monastic house, Barking Abbey and was long known as All Hallows Barking Church. It stands on the site of Roman buildings and incorporates Roman materials in its Saxon fabric. The chancel is fourteenth century, the aisles fifteenth, the tower seventeenth and the crypt and steeple twentieth. William Penn was christened here in 1644. In 1666 Pepys watched the Great Fire from the tower and naval hero Admiral Penn saved the church from the flames by demolishing the buildings around it. John Quincy Adams, later sixth President of the United States, was married here in 1797. The many treasures of All Hallows include three Saxon crosses, seventeen brasses, dated 1389-1651, a font-cover by Gibbons and the 'Toc H' Lamp of Maintenance.

26. All Hallows-by-the-Tower in the 18th century.

27. (Below) St Bartholomew the Great, West Smithfield, the oldest church building in London, containing the remains of the Augustinian priory founded in 1123.

The immense nave of St Bartholomew-the-Great was pulled down at the Dissolution but the Norman choir was handed over to parishioners, who had the tower replaced in 1628 and leased out most of the surviving monastic buildings. The crypt served as store for coal and wine, while the Lady Chapel was split into houses and workshops. Restoration was undertaken in 1863-5 by the youthful Aston Webb, future architect of the Victoria and Albert Museum. Its monuments include the tombs of Rahere and of Sir Walter Mildmay, founder of that nursery of Puritan divines, Emmanuel College, Cambridge.

St Andrew Undershaft certainly dates back to the twelfth century but the main structure of the present building is from 1532, modified by major restorations in 1634, 1726 and 1876. The church takes its unusual name from the Cornhill maypole erected outside its south door until the custom was discontinued after the 'Evil May Day' anti-Flemish apprentice riots of 1517. A memorial records that Holbein, court painter

28. *The diminutive church of St Ethelburga in Bishopsgate, rebuilt in the 15th century and later fronted by shops. It was virtually destroyed by an IRA bomb in 1993.*

29. *The 17th-century gates leading to St Olave, Hart Street, which sport skulls, crossbones and spikes.*

to Henry VIII, was probably a parishioner and may be buried here. Historian John Stow certainly is (see p43). The celebrated seventeenth-century 'monarchs' window' which was once the glory of the west end of the nave was blown out by the IRA bomb which blasted St Mary Axe in 1992.

Nearby St Helen's Bishopsgate suffered similarly from the Bishopsgate explosion of the following year but was restored by Quinlan Terry. St Helen was the mother of Constantine, Rome's first Christian emperor and the church was first recorded in 1150, shortly after Geoffrey of Monmouth claimed her as the daughter of (Old King) Coel, legendary ruler of Colchester. She was in fact born in what is now north-western Turkey but she did marry a Roman general, Constantius Chlorus, who led an expedition to London to overthrow a local usurper. Legend also credited her with finding the remains of the True Cross. Long a nunnery and parish church combined, St Helen's came to be known as 'the Westminster Abbey of the City' on account of its proliferation of monuments. Sir John Crosby and Sir Thomas Gresham (both see p35) are both buried here.

Tiny St Ethelburga's, barely a hundred yards away, having survived both Fire and Blitz, was reduced to rubble by the Bishopsgate blast. Its unique dedication, to Erkenwald's sister, Abbess of Barking, implies a Saxon foundation but it was first recorded in 1250 as Adelburga-the-Virgin and substantially re-

30. *The fourth St Paul's Cathedral, begun in Norman times, was larger and higher than today's building. The spire, struck by lightning in 1447 and rebuilt fifteen years later, was said to be almost 500' high – nearly as high as today's Telecom Tower.*

built in 1411. It was here that explorer Henry Hudson and his crew took their last communion in 1607 before setting out on their fatal voyage in search of the North-West Passage.

St Olave, Hart Street, dates from *c*.1450. The macabre skulls on its churchyard gate inspired Dickens to dub it "St. Ghastly Grim" in his *Uncommercial Traveller*. Named for the patron saint of Norway, the church retains a strong Norwegian connection and after post-blitz restoration was re-dedicated in 1954 by King Haakon VII, who worshipped here during his war-time exile. Like All Hallows, St Olave's was saved from the Great Fire by Admiral Penn. Pepys worshipped here while working at the Navy Office in Seething Lane round the corner and erected a monument to his wife Elizabeth, who pre-deceased him by thirty years. Both are buried here within the sanctuary.

St Sepulchre-without-Newgate is the largest parish church in the City and there has been a church here since at least 1137, when it was designated to the English 'St Edmund-King-and-Martyr'. The name change was probably inspired by the Crusades and the consequent knowledge that in Jerusalem the Church of the Holy Sepulchre stood outside the north-west gate. Most of the structure dates from the

fifteenth century but damage during the Great Fire required complete internal rebuilding. In 1555, vicar John Rogers became one of the first 'Smithfield Martyrs' when he refused to recant his Protestant faith. Captain John Smith, adventurer and effective founder of Virginia, is buried here and commemorated by a memorial plaque and a window. The south aisle is the memorial chapel of the City's own regiment, the Royal Fusiliers, and the railings around the churchyard are painted in their colours.

OLD ST PAUL'S
The second St Paul's was destroyed by Vikings in 961 and its successor burned down in 1087. The fourth cathedral stood at the heart of a complex of buildings which included a separate parish church, bishop's palace, school and campanile bell tower. During the Reformation the cathedral deteriorated. The nave was used as a short cut and a shopping mall and in 1561 the roof and spire were destroyed by fire. The roof was replaced but the spire was not. In 1628 Inigo Jones was asked to build an impressive, if incongruous, neo-classical portico along its west facade. The civil wars then cut short further refurbishment.

A Place of Merchants

COSMPOLITAN COMMERCE

Bede, the first historian of the English, writing around 731, refers to London as "the mart of many nations resorting to it by land and sea." By Norman times the City had acquired permanent commercial communities of Danes, French and Jews – whence Old Jewry and Jewry Street. Merchants of the powerful Hanseatic League, which managed the commercial interests of a confederation of German and Scandinavian trading cities, are mentioned as early as the tenth century and by 1157 had a permanent headquarters, the Steelyard, on Upper Thames Street where Cannon Street station now stands. Flemings handled the trade in fine wool, England's main export, destined for the cloth-making towns of Flanders and northern Italy. Gascons dealt with the important wine trade with Bordeaux. Other groups distinguished by contemporaries included Picards, Spaniards and Scots.

In the course of the thirteenth century, through forced loans and fines, the City's Jewish community was squeezed dry by its nominal protector, the Crown, and finally expelled altogether in 1290, not to be readmitted until Cromwell's time, in 1656. Their unenviable place was taken by the Lombards.

The presence of commercially powerful ethnic minorities by no means guaranteed multi-cultural harmony. The Hanse merchants took care to stay walled up in the Steelyard, prudently refusing even to join in with the locals at their sports, lest rough games lead to rough words and rougher blows. In 1308 Edward II was obliged to warn the citizenry on the eve of his coronation that discourtesy to foreign visitors would bring the offender a year and a day in gaol and confiscation of his entire property.

CITY COMPANIES

If international commerce was largely in foreign hands, domestic business was closely regulated by increasingly powerful guilds, which became formalised as royally chartered legal entities, whose leading members could be distinguished on ceremonial occasions by the distinctive and elaborate livery they wore. Originating in religious fraternities, dating from Saxon times, the livery companies enrolled all persons practising their particular trade or craft. Maintaining their spiritual aspect by organising processions and feasts on the day of their patron saint and guaranteeing a decent turn-out at the marriages,

31. An eighteenth-century depiction of steel bars being weighed at the Steelyard, the Hanseatic trading enclave on the site of today's Cannon Street station.

32. *The busiest place in London was probably the Custom House on Lower Thames Street. This building, probably the third on the site, was destroyed in the Great Fire of 1666. The first known customs duty was imposed in AD979. Customs officers were responsible for imposing duty on all the ships which came into the Pool of London. So congested did the port become that ships could be anchored in the river for weeks on end.*

christenings and funerals of their members, they also combined the functions of technical college, trading standards authority, social security system and dining club. Through fines, expulsion and rotation of office the livery companies kept their members in order and from their upper ranks provided the City's governing elite. In a volatile city whose prosperity was constantly threatened by the chances of war, epidemic or famine, at home or abroad, and whose cohesion was constantly challenged by the endless trickle of immigrants from beyond its walls, the livery companies provided a valuable framework of stability.

Collectively, the City companies, at the height of their influence from the fourteenth to the sixteenth centuries, could be immensely powerful, especially in the face of a threat to their common interests. But they were also in keen rivalry with one another. Precedence was regarded as a vital issue and was formally codified by the Court of Aldermen in 1514. The distinction between those who made a physical product and those who were dealers in goods remained an enduring one. The merchants were normally the wealthier and it should come as no surprise that the 'Great Twelve' Companies were headed by the Mercers (1), Grocers (2), Drapers (3) and Fishmongers (4). A sample of 268 persons who held the office of alderman between 1200 and 1334 reveals that seventy-nine were dealers in wool, sixty-five in cloth and another sixty-five in wine, these three trades thus accounting for three-quarters of the total.

Mergers and takeovers profoundly reshaped the City's institutional landscape over the centuries as the armourers absorbed first the blacksmiths then the makers of helmets, repairers of armour and finally workers in brass and copper and the blacksmiths re-established themselves by joining with the spurriers and the fullers and shearers joined to become the clothworkers and so on. During the seventeenth century new companies were chartered to recognise such trades as the makers of clocks, coaches, felt, glass, guns, machine-knitted goods, needles, playing cards, spectacles, tin plate, tobacco pipes and wheels. After the incorporation of the fan-makers in 1709, no new companies were chartered until the airline pilots and air navigators were recognised in 1929. Except in a few cases, such as the Goldsmiths, Vintners and Fishmongers, the livery companies largely lost their monopoly powers to regulate their businesses by the eighteenth century but continued to administer a vast number of charities and to provide recruits to man the infrastructure of City government.

MERCHANT ADVENTURERS

As the livery companies were beginning to pass their peak a new form of business organisation bustled onto the City scene – the joint-stock company, a risk-sharing device for mobilising capital to finance trade with distant markets. The Muscovy Company dealt with Russia, the Guinea Company with west Africa, the Levant Company with the eastern littoral of the Mediterranean. The Virginia Company pioneered the European settlement of the future United States, as the Hudson's Bay Company, in pursuit of pelts, opened up the Canadian north-west. Mightiest of all grew the East India Company which, brutally driven out of the lucrative spice trade of south-east Asia by their Dutch rivals, became *de facto* ruler of the Indian sub-continent. The global nature of London's commerce is strikingly revealed by the nature of the jeweller's stock known as 'the Cheapside Hoard' which was probably buried during the troubled 1640s and rediscovered by accident in 1912; it contains garnets from India, turquoises from Persia and emeralds from Colombia.

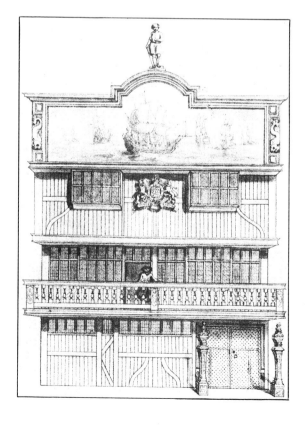

33. (Above) The hall of the Clothworkers' Company, rebuilt after the Great Fire of 1666. The first hall of the 'Shearmen', a component of the Clothworkers' Company, was built in Mincing Lane in c.1472.

34. (Right) The East India Company headquarters in 1711, formerly the 'great mansion house' of Sir William Craven. The house was rebuilt in 1726.

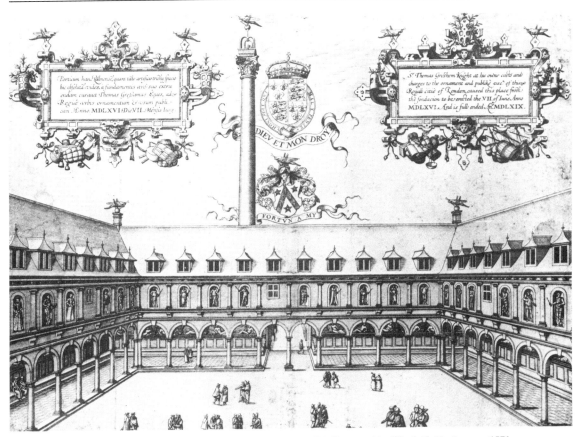

35. *The first Royal Exchange, built by Sir Thomas Gresham. It was officially opened by Elizabeth I in January 1571.*

CONFIDENT CITY

The foreign merchants who had so long handled Britain's external trade found themselves increasingly elbowed aside. London merchants became confident to operate abroad. William Caxton (?1422-91), who brought printing to London, spent almost a quarter of a century in Bruges, latterly as governor of all the English merchants operating in the Low Countries. Between 1466 and 1475 grocer Sir John Crosby built himself a fine mansion in Bishopsgate on the basis of a fortune he had made as "ane of the first that ventrid into Spayn". The privileges of the Hanse merchants were revoked in 1551 and they were expelled altogether in 1598. The sack of Antwerp by the Spanish in 1568 severely damaged a major rival. The Thirty Years War of 1618-48 set back the economy of central Europe for decades afterwards. By the late seventeenth century even the Dutch had been pushed off their perch by a combination of discriminatory legislation and open warfare.

The increasing self-confidence of the City was visibly symbolised by the construction of the Royal Exchange as a combination of bourse and up-market shopping mall. Its creator, Thomas Gresham, arms-dealer, commercial spy, currency reformer and confidential financial adviser to the Crown, raised subscriptions from 750 leading Londoners to buy the site but paid for the building entirely out of his own huge fortune. Gresham laid the first brick personally in June 1566. Elizabeth I conferred the dignity 'Royal' on it in January 1571.

The increasing scale and complexity of the City's commerce was matched by the emergence of new financial services as goldsmiths evolved from passive deposit-takers, offering physical security for the wealth of their clients, to active bankers, advancing credit on the security of assets at their disposal. Marine and, later, life insurance became available thanks to the advances in mathematics which were such a marked feature of a century which embraced not only Napier and Newton but the more practically-minded Sir William Petty (1623-87), the pioneer of comparative statistics, who laid the foundations of actuarial science. The culmination of these developments was the foundation in 1694 of the Bank of England –

36. Sir Thomas Gresham, founder of the Royal Exchange. In his Worthies of England Thomas Fuller credited him with founding "two stately Fabricks, the Old Exchange, a kind of Colledge for merchants, and Gresham Colledge, a kind of Exchange for Scholars."

37. William Paterson (1658-1719), founder of the Bank of England. He resigned from the board of the Bank a year after founding it and lost his fortune and family in the disastrous Scottish scheme to settle the Isthmus of Panama.

SIC VOS NON VOBIS

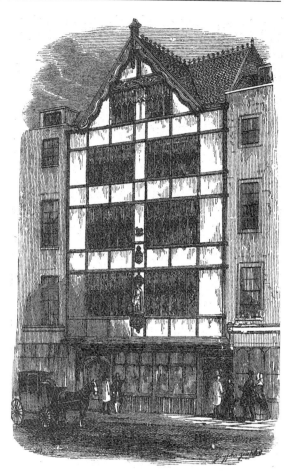

38. Crosby Hall, Bishopsgate, the mansion built by Sir John Crosby, a wealthy grocer, in 1466-75. Richard of Gloucester was living here at the time of the murder of the two princes in the Tower of London. The remains of the house were moved to Danvers Street, Chelsea in 1909-10.

invented by a Scotsman, William Paterson, and headed by the son of a Huguenot, Sir John Houblon, to finance the wars of a Dutch king, William III.

Such cosmopolitanism was the inevitable accompaniment of a global commerce which would determine the fortunes of the City and its inhabitants henceforth.

39. Smithfield cattle market in the 1820s, by Thomas H. Shepherd.

MARKETS

Billingsgate, as famed for foul language as for fish, was already long-established by 979 when provision was made for the payment of tolls or customs by vessels unloading there. For centuries it was also a landing-point for corn and other foodstuffs as well as fish. The present handsome building, designed by Sir Horace Jones, opened in 1877 and finally closed in 1982.

Smithfield had a noted Friday horse fair by the twelfth century which developed into a general livestock market. In 1638 the City Corporation formally established it as a cattle market with a Royal Charter but it became notorious for filthiness and disorderly behaviour. The sale of live animals finally ceased in 1855 and was relocated in Islington, and a new market building, modelled on Paxton's Crystal Palace and designed by Sir Horace Jones, was erected between 1851 and 1866, complete with an underground railway link with King's Cross. Extended in 1875, 1899 and 1963, it was entirely refurbished in 1993-5.

The Stocks market was established in the thirteenth century by Lord Mayor Henry le Walleis where the Mansion House now stands. Sellers of bad fish or flesh were pilloried on the spot. Rebuilt many times, from 1675 onwards it featured an equestrian statue of Charles II (which had originally been made to honour Poland's national hero John Sobieski). Strype described it as "surpassing all other markets in London"

but in 1737, to make way for the construction of the Mansion House, the market was removed to a bridge over the Fleet Ditch and renamed Fleet market. It was finally cleared away from there in 1826-30 to allow the construction of Farringdon Street.

Leadenhall market, dating from the fourteenth century as a general provision market, later sold herbs, wool, cloth, leather and cutlery as well. The present buildings, designed by Sir Horace Jones, date from 1881.

Honey Lane market was established for the sale of meat and provisions after the Great Fire, to replace the old Cheapside markets. Rebuilt by George Dance the Younger in 1787-88, it was cleared to make way for the building of the City of London School.

Spitalfields, a market for vegetables, was opened in 1682. The present buildings, which are now used for a general market, mainly for clothes and organic foods, were largely built by Robert Horner, a self-made man who had once worked there as a porter. Bought and modernised by the City Corporation in 1920, it incorporated such features as heated cellars for ripening bananas.

Rag Fair, a market rather than a fair, was located in Rosemary Lane (renamed Royal Mint Street in 1850). As the name implies, it specialised in the tattiest cast-off clothing. A similar, equally grim, market could be found in Cutler Street, off Houndsditch.

40. *The Skin Market at Leadenhall; published in 1825.*

41. *Billingsgate Market in the 18th century.*

42 & 43: *A London merchant's wife and daughter in the 17th century; drawings by Wenceslaus Hollar.*

44. *(top left) Billingsgate market, by Augustus Callcott, 1898.*

45. *(bottom left) At the lower end of the market trade - a Jewish old clothes seller, depicted in Mayhew's* London Labour and the London Poor.

46. *(above) The type of shop front that has disappeared from the City. This was in the City portion of Artillery Lane, off Bishopsgate. It is pictured in the early 1920s.*

47. *Leadenhall Market, as depicted by Pugin and Rowlandson in Ackermann's* Microcosm of London *c1808*

48. *Stocks Market, on the site of today's Mansion House. It featured the equestrian statue of Charles II, which had been adapted from one depicting the Polish hero, John Sobieski.*

Stow's City

THE PRICE OF THE PAST

John Stow (1525-1605) is London's first true historian, a devoted antiquarian who both quarried ancient sources and chronicled, somewhat acerbically, the great transformations of his own times. Stow came from a line of tallow-chandlers but himself worked as a tailor, being admitted to the freedom of the Merchant Taylors in 1547. He set up business near the well at Aldgate and prospered enough to allow him to start collecting books and write in his spare time. His first publication was an edition of Chaucer (1561), followed by a series of outlines of English history. By his late forties Stow, despite the displeasure of his family, was devoting himself to working on the history of London full time. His zeal verged on the obsessive, as he himself subsequently confessed, acknowledging that his magnum opus "hath cost me many a weary mile's travel, many a hard earned penny and pound, and many a cold winter night's study." And all this without the benefit of either a formal scholarly training or even the financial support and encouragement of a wealthy patron. The fruit of Stow's labours was the *Survey of London*, first published in 1598. For this first edition he received just three pounds, plus forty copies of the book. It reprinted within a year and a second edition appeared in 1603. But success, such as it was, came to Stow all too late.

His *Survey* had, indeed, cost the author dear, for in 1602 he was glad to accept an addition of two pounds annually to his existing pensions of eight pounds a year and in 1604 was granted letters patent by James I, allowing him to solicit 'voluntary contributions and kind gratuities.'

Stow "attempted the discovery of London, my native soil and Country" so that... "what London hath been of ancient time, men may here see, as what it is now every man doth behold." Stow, fortunately for succeeding historians of London, limited himself to no single method of research but visited churches in person, pestered livery companies to let him pore through their records, noted down the reminiscences of aged neighbours and acquaintances and drew on his own personal memories and observations. When even Stow's considerable persistence could not prevail, he had his own way of getting back at the uncooperative. The Vintners' Company, who denied him access to their archive, he consigned to historical oblivion by simply omitting them

49. *The effigy of John Stow in the church of St Andrew Undershaft. Each year, as a tribute to London's first historian, the Lord Mayor replaces the quill pen in Stow's hand.*

TUDOR TRANSFORMATION

Many of Stow's anecdotes and comments concern the physical transformations which had so changed the City in his own century as a consequence of its mushroom growth. The London he was born into had a population of about 50,000; by the time he died it was 200,000. One particularly vivid example of 'development' concerned a property of his own father in the Throgmorton Street area which had the misfortune to lie adjacent to a holding of Henry VIII's overbearing chief minister, Thomas Cromwell (?1485-1540):

My father had a garden there, and a house standing close to his south pale; this house they loosed from the ground and bare upon rollers into my father's garden twenty-two feet, ere my father heard thereof; no warning was given him, nor other answer when

50. Aldgate Pump at the beginning of this century at the junction of Leadenhall and Fenchurch Streets. Aldgate Well is mentioned as early as the reign of King John.

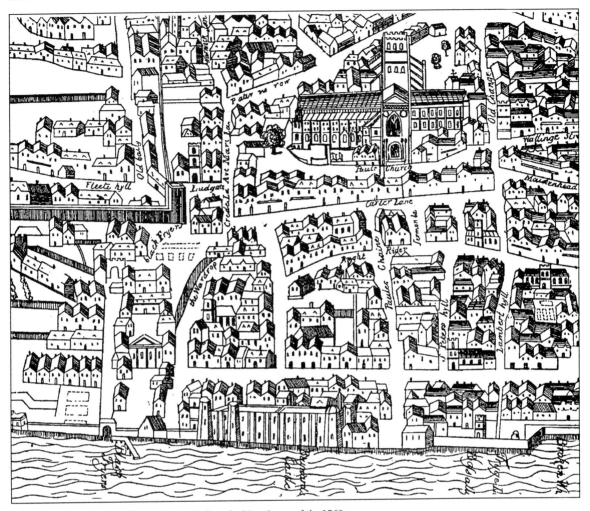

51. The neighbourhood of St Paul's, depicted on the 'Agas' map of the 1560s.

he spake to the surveyors of that work but that their master Sir Thomas commanded them so to do.

Having suffered such treatment, it is little wonder that Stow should chronicle the misfortunes of the mighty with a whiff of malice:

Sir John Champneis, Alderman and Mayor.... built a high tower of brick, the first I ever heard of in any private man's house to overlook his neighbours in the city. But this delight of his eye was punished with blindness some years before his death.

As an old man Stow was, unsurprisingly, prone to nostalgia, recalling the London of his childhood as a semi-rustic idyll. Writing of the Minories, where a nunnery of Minoresses once stood, he recorded that:

On the south side thereof was sometime a farm.... at the which farm I myself in my youth have fetched many a halfpenny worth of milk, and never less than three ale pints for a halfpenny in

summer, nor less than one ale quart for a halfpenny in winter, always hot from the kine.

Doubtless these indulgent reminscences were provoked by the sprawling, stinking slums proliferating eastwards, just beyond his own doorstep. Despite a decree of 1580 which had banned any housebuilding within three miles of any City gate, the road leading up to Aldgate was "pestered with cottages", while riverside Wapping had become "a continual street or filthy straight passage with alleys of small tenements". Again:

(Hog Lane).... within these forty years, had on both sides fair hedgerows of elm trees, with bridges and easy stiles to pass over into the pleasant fields, very commodious for citizens therein to walk, shoot and otherwise to recreate and refresh their dulled spirits in the sweet and wholesome air, which is now within a few

52. *One of the most striking houses erected in London in the early Stuart period was that of London merchant, Sir Paul Pindar, in Bishopsgate. It was demolished in 1890 to make way for Liverpool Street station, but some of the frontage was saved and is situated today in the shop at the Victoria & Albert Museum.*

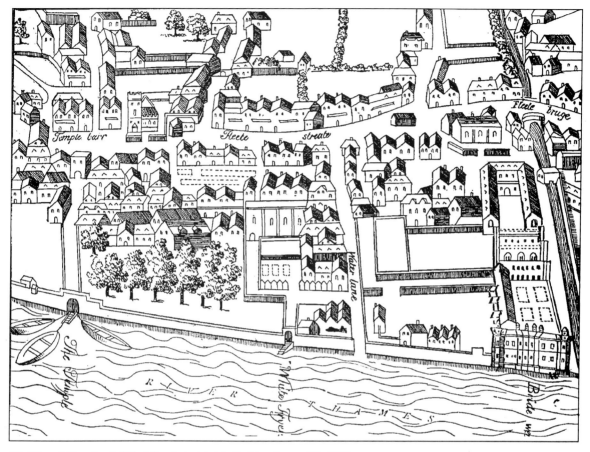

53. *The neighbourhood of Fleet Street, depicted in the 'Agas' map of the 1590s.*

years made a continual building throughout.... and the fields on either side be turned into garden plots.... bowling alleys and such like.

Courtiers and officials were moving westwards, along the Strand and towards Whitehall, leaving behind the City's din to enjoy pleasant gardens and refined company. Tradesmen moved eastwards towards Whitechapel, to evade the regulations of the City companies and find cheaper premises where they could pollute both air and water without offend-ing powerful neighbours.

After his death Stow was buried in St Andrew Undershaft where, shortly afterwards, his widow raised an imposing marble and alabaster monument to his memory. Poised, pen in hand, he frowns in concentration, surrounded by his beloved books. The City honours his memory with an annual service, during which the incumbent Lord Mayor replaces his quill with a new one.

54. *A Lord Mayor and Aldermen during the reign of Queen Elizabeth I.*

Pomp and Ceremony

THE LORD MAYOR

The Lord Mayor of London is the City's first citizen, its Chief Magistrate, Admiral of the Port of London, Chancellor of City University and Chairman of both the Court of Aldermen and the Court of Common Council. Within the City boundaries the Lord Mayor ranks second only to the Sovereign and ahead even of Princes of the royal blood.

The office of Mayor is not as old as that of Sheriff, but dates from the reign of Richard I (1189-99), whose passion was war. The crusader king, who spent less than six months of his reign in England, is said to have declared that he would sell London itself if he could find a buyer. Royal financial embarrassment has ever been the City's opportunity and recognition of the mayoralty was the price extracted for supporting Richard's foreign adventures. The first holder of the office, Henry FitzAylwin, was spared the tiresome nuisance of annual re-election and held power from 1192 until his death in 1212. His successor, Roger FitzAlan, took advantage of the difficulties of Richard's successor, John (1199-1216) to extract a charter confirming the right of London's citizens to elect their own Chief Magistrate. Only a few weeks later John was obliged to concede even more limitations on the royal prerogative by accepting the baronial demands enshrined in Magna Carta. FitzAlan was the only commoner among the baronial negotiators – a remarkable testimony to his unique standing – and, commoner or not, styled himself by his surname only, like a peer. Although the term 'Lord Mayor' is referred to as early as 1283, it was not habitually used until the 1540s.

Probably the most famous Lord Mayor of all, and certainly the only one to be hallowed in English folklore, was Dick Whittington. He certainly did exist and held office no less than four times – in 1397 (twice), 1406 and 1419. But almost every other element in the popular legend attached to him since the seventeenth century is either false or a distortion. He was never penniless. There is no record that he was ever knighted. And if he ever had a 'cat', it was probably a type of boat used in the coastal coal trade from Newcastle. Whittington was the third son of a wealthy Gloucestershire merchant and had the good sense to marry his boss's daughter. He eventually became master of the Mercers' Company and loaned money to three kings, allegedly throwing Henry V's bond for £60,000 into the fire at a banquet to celebrate the king's stupendous victory at Agincourt. Whittington's larger-than-life persona is probably a by-product of his prodigal generosity, which included sponsoring a 120-seat public lavatory in Vintry, gen-

55. Richard Whittington

erous donations to the libraries of Guildhall and Christchurch, Greyfriars, paying for flooring and windows in Guildhall and refurbishing Bart's Hospital and Newgate prison.

The only Lord Mayor to have been honoured with a statue was William Beckford. Born in Jamaica, he inherited an immense fortune, accumulated through plantation slavery, which enabled him to become a fearless defender of English liberty. Holding office in 1762 and 1769, Beckford was a staunch supporter of the unscrupulous and manipulative John Wilkes in his long-running campaign against allegedly oppressive government. On one occasion, when a Common Council petition against governmental interference in parliamentary elections was ignored by the Crown, Beckford had the temerity to give an astonished George III an impromptu lecture on the fundamentals of the British constitution, until the monarch "stood speechless and there was trouble and agitation among his ministers and courtiers."

Other unique Lord Mayors include American-born Barlow Trecothick who, on the eve of the American Revolution, was both Lord Mayor and MP for the City; Belgian Polydor de Keyser, who started as a waiter, became the City's first Catholic Lord Mayor since the Reformation and founded a luxurious hotel,

56. *The Lord Mayor's procession approaching Westminster. Painting by Sir Henry Tulse, 1683.*

named for himself, at Blackfriars, where Unilever House has stood since 1930; George Swan Nottage, who, dying in office in 1884, was accorded the unique customary honour of burial in St Paul's cathedral; and Mary Donaldson who in 1983 became the City's first ever lady Lord Mayor.

THE LORD MAYOR'S SHOW

The charter granted to the City in 1215 required its mayor to swear fealty to the king or to judges acting on his behalf. Unlike the 'silent change', during which the emblems of office pass from one mayor to his successor with the most discreet solemnity, the annual procession of a new incumbent to profess his loyalty, rather than paring ceremony to its minimum, for centuries did the opposite, becoming an ever more extravagant display of civic pomp and personal ostentation. The first record of aldermen accompanying the mayor is in 1378. By 1401 minstrels had been added to his retinue. From 1422 onwards the journey to Westminster Hall, the seat of the highest courts of the land, was undertaken by water in a barge of Venetian magnificence. After kitchens were added to Guildhall in 1501 a mayoral banquet became an essential feature of the proceedings.

Specially commissioned pageants were sponsored to amuse the onlookers. In 1553 Henry Machyn, an undertaker, recorded the scene as the cavalcade landed on its way back from Westminster:

My Lord Mayor landed at Baynards Castle and then came trumpeters blowing, then came a devil and after came the bachelors all in livery and scarlet hoods, and then came the pageant of St John Baptist gorgeously with goodly speeches and then came all the King's trumpeters ... and then the Crafts and then my Lord Mayor and good henchmen and then all the Aldermen and Sheriffs and so to dinner.

In exceptional circumstances, during outbreaks of plague and under the Puritans, the show did not take place. In 1661, shortly after its restoration, along with the monarch, Pepys, no radical or killjoy, recorded sniffily of the pageants he saw on Cheapside "which were many and I believe good, for such kind of things, but in themselves poor and absurd". But, despite its suspension during the Great Plague and for some years after the Great Fire, the City's most splendid day continued to draw the crowds, as Ned Ward described indignantly in 1706:

Whilst my Friend and I were thus staring at the Spectators, much more than the Show, the Pageants were advanc'd within our view, upon which such a Tide of Mob over-flow'd the Place we stood ... For my own part ... I was so closely Imprisoned between the Bums and Bellies of the Multitude, that I was almost squeez'd as flat as a Napkin in a Press.

A Swiss visitor, Cesar de Saussure, writing in the 1720s, found the popular mood positively intimidating:

The populace is particularly insolent and rowdy, turning into lawless freedom the great liberty it enjoys. As these times it is almost dangerous for an honest man and more particularly for a foreigner, if at all well dressed, to walk in the streets, for he runs the great risk of being insulted by the vulgar populace, which is the most cursed brood in existence.

A stylish new element was added in 1757 when, for the first time, the Lord Mayor travelled in the elaborate coach which has been used ever since. Designed

57. Guildhall in the 1920s.

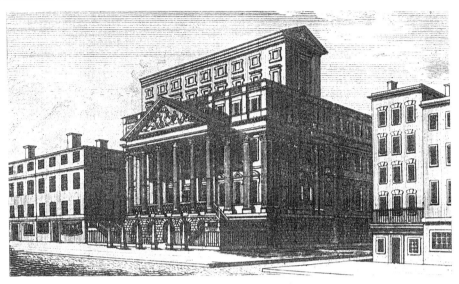

58. *The Mansion House; published in Chamberlain's* History of London, 1770.

by Sir Robert Taylor (1714-88), who was later responsible for the elegant Court Room of the Bank of England, it featured richly-painted emblematic panels (probably by Cipriani) but no springs and, until 1951, no brakes either. From the 1850s onwards, as the City became more a place of work and less a place of residence, the procession came to feature displays and floats celebrating its role in commerce and explaining its contribution to the economic life of the nation. The state barge was used for the last time in 1856 and from 1883 the procession was much shortened after the judges vacated Westminster Hall in favour of the new Royal Courts of Justice at the junction of the Strand and Fleet Street.

GUILDHALL

Guildhall is the seat of the City's government and the setting for much official hospitality, especially to visiting heads of state. Of medieval halls only Westminster Hall is larger and Guildhall has the additional attraction of a large surviving undercroft. A Guildhall is referred to as early as 1128 but the present building, by John Croxton, dates from between 1411 and 1439, and has survived destruction by fire in both 1666 and 1940. The entrance facade on the south side was substantially altered by George Dance the Younger in 1788-9. A library, by Sir Horace Jones, was added in 1870-73 and extensive offices by Sir Giles Gilbert Scott between the 1950s and 1970s.

MANSION HOUSE

Traditionally Mayors lived in their own houses and entertained there or in the hall of their livery company. An official residence for the Lord Mayor was proposed in John Evelyn's plan for the rebuilding of the City after the Great Fire but it was not until 1735, after several abortive attempts to get the scheme under way, that it was finally decided to clear the old Stocks Market and begin building. Responsibility for the design was given to George Dance (1700-68), Clerk of the City Works. Bowing to current taste for Palladian style, Dance probably based his designs on the huge mansion at Wanstead built by Colen Campbell for City tycoon Sir Josiah Child. Begun in 1739 and ready for occupation in 1752, the Mansion House was hailed as "a Hallelujah chorus in stone". The pediment housed a sculptural frieze, designed by Sir Robert Taylor, in which an emblematic figure of London tramples Envy while leading in Plenty under the approving gaze of Father Thames. The external appearance of the Mansion House then differed significantly from what it looks like now thanks to the roof-level extrusions Dance added to give extra height to the two main public rooms. These were irreverently nick-named the Mayor's Nest and Noah's Ark. In 1794-5 George Dance the Younger (1741-1825) who had succeeded to his father's office, roofed over the central courtyard to create a new saloon and removed Noah's Ark. The Mayor's Nest went in 1842, when the Ball Room was reconstructed. In 1931 the Mansion House was substantially refurnished in its original style, sweeping away many Victorian alterations. A further major overhaul was undertaken sixty years later.

Plague and Fire

HOLOCAUST

The Great Plague of 1665 truly was, in Roy Porter's graphic phrase, "a disaster of nuclear proportions". Plague in itself was a regular enough occurrence. In the six decades since the accession of James I there had only been four entirely plague-free years. What was extraordinary about the outbreak of 1665 was its sheer magnitude. Official 'Bills of Mortality' put the death-toll at 68,576 over a period of eighteen months but parish clerks often falsified their returns to minimise panic, as one admitted to Pepys – "There died nine this week, though I have returned only six." The true figure was probably a third as high again as officially recorded, representing at least a sixth of the population of the entire metropolis – or as many as the inhabitants of Norwich, Bristol, Newcastle, York and Exeter added together.

It began in April 1665, well outside the City proper, in St Giles-in-the-Fields, already a semi-rural slum to the south of newly-developing Bloomsbury. Not until late May was there a plague death in the City itself, at Cornhill. A foetid June then helped the infection spread rapidly. It raged most fiercely in the squalid, overcrowded districts fringing the City walls – Holborn, Shoreditch, Finsbury, Whitechapel and Southwark – where foul privies, putrefying garbage and scavenging poultry and pigs provided a utopian environment for the plague-bearing black rat. Pepys noted thankfully that in the last week of June only four of those who had died had done so in the City itself "which is great blessing to us." Those who could afford to do so, fled – including Charles II and his court. His Majesty's more dutiful subjects, including the Lord Mayor and the conscientious, if fearful, Pepys, remained, as did many devoted priests, doctors and apothecaries.

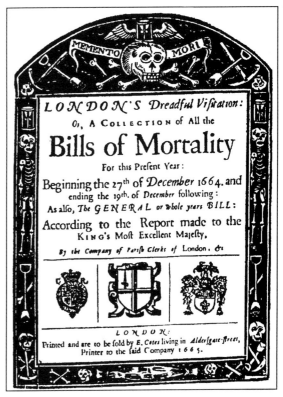

60. *Title page to a collection of the Bills of Mortality for the Great Plague year of 1665.*

Some ten thousand Londoners marooned themselves on boats in the river; their survival rate was the highest in the capital. Official policy was to order non-residents to quit the City, to light fires in the streets to 'purge' the air and to quarantine sufferers by nailing them up in their houses for forty days. Also to exterminate dogs and cats, which were believed to be carriers of the contagion; this was, in fact, counter-

59. *A scene from the plague year of 1630.*

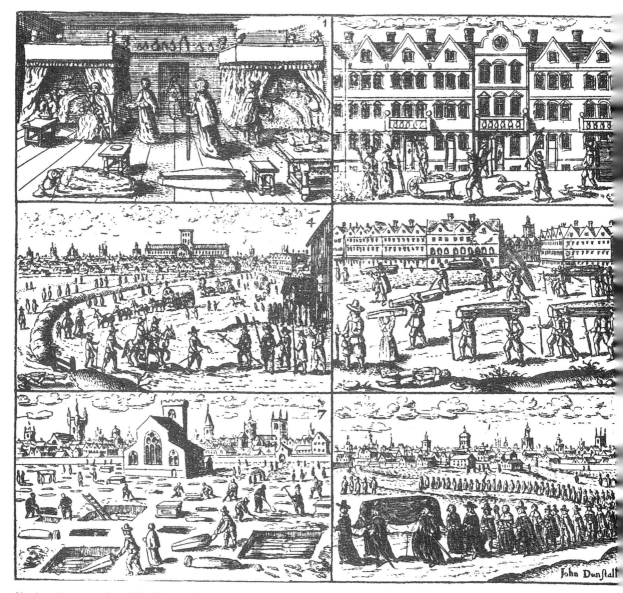

61. *A contemporary broadside of scenes from the Great Plague in London, 1665.*

One of the most moving contemporary accounts of the Plague is that of Samuel Pepys. He records in his diary of 8 August:

'The streets empty all the way now, even to London, which is a sad sight. And to Westminster Hall, where talking, hearing very sad stories from Mrs. Mumford; among others of Michell's son's family. And poor Will, that used to sell us ale at the Hall door, his wife and three children dead, all I think in a day. So home, through the City again, wishing I may have taken no ill in going; but I will go, I think, no more thither.

On 15 August, he notes:

It was dark before I could get home, and so land at Churchyard Stairs where, to my great trouble, I met a dead corpse of the Plague, in the narrow alley just bringing down a little pair of stairs. But I thank God I was not much disturbed by it. However, I shall beware of being late abroad again.

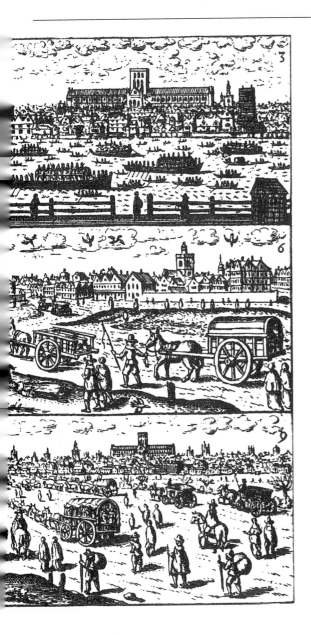

productive as they were the only effective check on the rats which were the carriers of plague-bearing fleas. By July the weekly death-toll had reached a thousand. By August that figure had doubled. The peak came in September, when 12,000 died in just seven days. By then mass-burials in lime-pits had become the norm and the local economy had virtually collapsed. Servants and apprentices whose masters had died or fled were left to fend for themselves by begging, mugging or looting. Newcastle colliers refused to put in to unload coal. Grass literally grew in the streets. Pepys recorded in October that he went "to Lumbard Streete but can get no money. So upon the Exchange, which is very empty." With the onset of cold weather in November the weekly harvest of corpses at last dipped below a thousand but not until February of the following year did the royal entourage deem it prudent to return from Oxford.

HEAVEN'S WRATH?

By the end of the hot summer of 1666 the close-packed wooden homes of Londoners were tinderbox-dry. On the night of 2 September a lethal spark was provided by a neglected oven in the bakeshop of the royal baker in Pudding Lane. Fanned by an unusually strong wind, the flames spread quickly to adjoining properties, including riverside warehouses and wharves packed with combustible timber, spars, ropes and barrels of tar and turpentine. Not only did these blaze mightily, they also cut off would-be firefighters from the only source of water sufficient to subdue the flames. Catastrophically, the City authorities were slow to grasp the scale of impending disaster. Awakened with the news, Lord Mayor Bludworth was memorably dismissive, sneering that "a woman might piss it out." It was Samuel Pepys himself, then resident in Seething Lane, who sped to Whitehall to report to the King in person. Charles acted decisively, sending orders that the Lord Mayor should pull down houses to create fire-breaks. It was a standard procedure but already too late. The population of the City was seized with panic, its residents fleeing with what valuables they could carry, as the flames, still fanned by a strong east wind, advanced menacingly westwards towards St Paul's itself, leaping whole streets, a wall of destruction up to three hundred feet high. Diarist John Evelyn's summarised the situation in brief compass – "The conflagration was so universal and the people so astonished that from the beginning... they hardly stirred to quench it, so as there was nothing heard or seen but crying out and lamentation, running about like distracted creatures.... God grant mine eyes never behold the like, who now saw above ten thousand houses, all in one flame."

Evelyn's 'ten thousand houses' sounds suspiciously like a rhetorical flourish but was actually short of the mark. Despite heroic efforts by the King himself and

On 20 August, on a visit to Brentford:
Told my bad news, and hear the Plague is round about them there. And to church, where a dull sermon and many Londoners. After church to my inn, and ate and drank, and so about seven o'clock by water, and got between nine and ten to Queenhithe, very dark; and I could not get my waterman to go elsewhere for fear of the Plague. Thence with a lantern, in great fear of meeting dead corpses, carrying to be buried; but, blessed be God! met none, but did see now and then a link, which is the mark of them, at a distance.

62. *A pre-Fire house in Leadenhall Street which escaped destruction. Close-packed against its neighbours and constructed almost entirely of wood, it illustrates why the blaze spread so rapidly. Drawn 1796 by John Thomas Smith.*

63. *Another pre-Fire house which survived the event. This house, drawn in 1808 by John Thomas Smith, was on the south side of London Wall.*

64. *The Great Fire of London 1666, depicted by an unknown artist.*

65. *Samuel Pepys, whose descriptions of the Plague and the Fire are unsensational and, for that reason, the most moving.*

Etiam periere Ruinæ

66. *The burning of St Paul's, as depicted by Wenceslaus Hollar.*

his brother James, Duke of York, commanding teams of sailors, by the time the fire had run its course almost four hundred acres had been reduced to smouldering ash within the City walls and over sixty acres outside. The heart of medieval London had been reduced to heaps of ashes, punctuated by occasional piles of scorched stone. Thirteen thousand houses were gone, leaving a hundred thousand Londoners homeless, many camped out under canvas in Moorfields. Eighty-seven churches had been gutted, plus the halls of forty-four livery companies and the City's landmark buildings – the Royal Exchange, the Custom House and St Paul's itself, with severe damage to Guildhall. But the loss of life had been negligible – just eight persons. A deranged Frenchman obligingly confessed to starting the fire and the Londoners obligingly hanged him. Popular bigotry blamed a Catholic plot. Religious zealots interpreted it as divine chastisement for the wanton profligacy of the restored Stuart court. A sober parliamentary enquiry went part way to supporting this view, indicting "the hand of God upon us, a great wind and the season so very dry."

RECONSTRUCTION
King Charles, ever the pragmatist, having issued decrees to organize emergency food-supplies and storage for valuables, agreed to sanction a national fast of atonement a month hence and also called for plans for a new London, grander and more gracious than ever. Wren, Evelyn, Hooke and others obliged within days with drafts of visionary schemes; but it was not to be. The Fleet never became a Venetian Grand Canal and the City's crazy-paving pattern of street-lines was more or less faithfully re-created. The 'Merry Monarch' was no Bourbon absolutist and had been but newly-restored to his throne. And, while many of the City's wealthier residents did relocate themselves ingratiatingly around the court in St James's and briefly fashionable Soho, (about 20,000 never returned), those who had lived 'above the shop' wanted that shop back in business rather than cash – which the Crown did not in any case have.

For once the legal profession showed itself in an exemplary light as a specially-constituted Fire Court, though hampered by the destruction of much documentation, speedily sorted out who owned what underneath the stinking, waist-high wasteland that stretched from the foreshore to Smithfield. Six 'Commissioners for Rebuilding the City of London' were appointed and Wren and Hooke made a preliminary survey of the burned-out area. New regulations led to the widening of over a hundred thoroughfares and the provision of proper gutters and pavements for the greater convenience and cleanliness of pedestrians.

67. *The Monument, erected in 1671-7 and designed by Christopher Wren and Robert Hooke.   The column, excluding the plinth and the superstructure above the capital, is 202ft high, the highest isolated stone monument in the world –
this is supposed to be the distance from the seat of the Great Fire in nearby Pudding Lane.   When built the Monument aligned with the old London Bridge.*

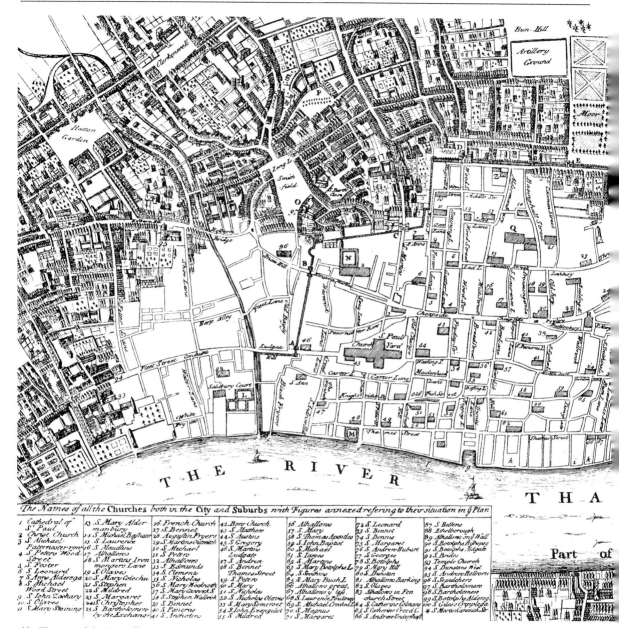

68. The area of the City affected by the Great Fire.

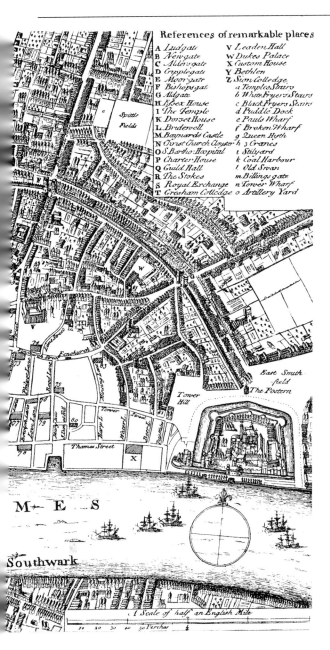

References of remarkable places

A	*Ludgate*	V	*Leaden Hall*
B	*Newgate*	W	*Dukes Palace*
C	*Aldersgate*	X	*Custom House*
D	*Cripplegate*	Y	*Bethlen*
E	*Moorgate*	Z	*Sion Colledge.*
F	*Bishopsgate*	a	*Temples Stairs*
G	*Aldgate*	b	*White Fryers Stairs*
H	*Essex House*	c	*Black Fryers Stairs*
I	*The Temple*	d	*Puddle Dock*
K	*Dorset House*	e	*Pauls Wharf*
L	*Bridewell*	f	*Broken Wharf*
M	*Baynards Castle*	h	*Cranes*
N	*Christ Church Cloyster*	g	*Queen Hyth*
O	*S. Bartho. Hospital*	i	*Stilyard*
P	*Charter House*	k	*Coal Harbour*
Q	*Guild Hall*	l	*Old Swan*
R	*The Stokes*	m	*Billings gate*
S	*Royal Exchange*	n	*Tower Wharf*
T	*Gresham Colledge*	o	*Artillery Yard*

69. *Sir Christopher Wren. City Surveyor, Robert Hooke, wrote of him "There scarce ever met in one man, in so great a perfection, such a Mechanical Hand, and so Philosophical a Mind."*

The Fleet was at least dredged and decently embanked. Several quays were improved and King Street and Queen Street laid out as completely new links between Guildhall and the Thames. Houses were to be built of brick or stone with walls of a minimum thickness. Those fronting onto main roads were to be four storeys high, those in 'streets and lanes of note' three high and only in by-ways just two. By 1669 Guildhall had been refurbished and by 1671 nine thousand dwellings had been rebuilt. In the same year construction of 'The Monument' began. It was completed in 1677, the year in which John Ogilby and William Morgan published their splendid new map of London, the first to be based on a truly scientific survey.

REFERENCES
1 Temple Barr
2 Fleet Conduit
3 S.t Dunstans in the West
4 Seargeants Inn
5 The New Channel
6 The Colledge of Physicians
7 8 S.t Pauls
9 10 } The two Sheriffs of London Houses
11 Mercers Chapel
12 Bow Church and the Arches
13 The Fountain in Grace church Street
14 S.t Dunstans in the East
15 Guild Hall
16 Chrits Hospital and Church
17 The Lord Mayors House
18 The Royal Exchange
19 The Trinity House
20 The Custom House & Admiralty Court
21 The Navy Office
22 Billings Gate
23 The Fish Market
24 Queen Hithe
25 Pauls Wharf
26 The Sluce
27 } Sessions House, Newgate Prison Publick Work House, & Bridewell
28 The Church Yards & Inns
29 The Key
30 Black Friers Church & Watling Street
31 The Tower
32 New-Gate
33 Alders-Gate
34 Cripple-Gate
35 Moor-Gate
36 Bishops-Gate
37 Ald-Gate
38 Charles-Gate
+ The several Parish Churches &c in Num.
• The Halls of the 12 Antient Companies
o The Publick Fountains .

The rest of the openings are for the Markets &c. And in the intermedial Squares and Areas, what narrower Streets shall be thought fit

70. *John Evelyn's plan for the reconstruction of the City. As with Wren's plan, Evelyn pressed for a monumental city, one that was laid out in straight lines, with landmark features at street intersections. His plan paid no regard to existing street patterns and land ownership and therefore could not be adopted.*

ST PAUL'S

Wren had been approached in 1663 to draw up plans for refurbishing St Paul's, then in a sadly dilapidated state after a decade of Puritan abuse. His radical solution – demolish and rebuild – was unacceptable. So were numerous of his draft schemes, until one was finally endorsed – just a week before the Great Fire ensured that demolition and rebuilding would be the only practicable course.

Wren initially wanted an equilateral Greek Cross ground-plan but this was far too alien for native taste. (St Stephen, Walbrook is said to represent a model of what it might have been.) Another effort, embodied in a 'Great Model', which cost three times his annual £200 fee, was also turned down, reducing the architect, quite literally, to tears. Finally, in 1675, a design was authorised by the sovereign's royal warrant which left Wren leeway "to make some variations rather ornamental than essential, as from time to time he should see proper."

Wren interpreted this discretion, to say the least, liberally, shortening the nave and dispensing altogether with the approved steeple in favour of a dome, an unprecedented feature in an English cathedral. Normally such a building was constructed and opened, section by section, starting at the east end.

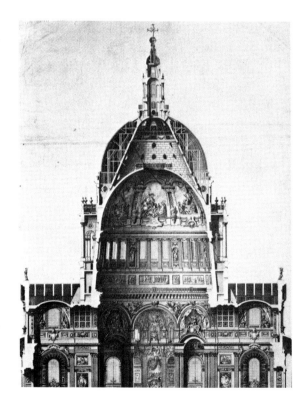

71. *Diagram published in 1755 displaying the method used by Wren to support the massive dome of St Paul's.*

72. *St Paul's seen at the end of one of London's narrow alleys, King's Head Passage. Painted by James S. Ogilvy, 1910.*

73. *St Dunstan's in the East, Idol Lane, which was damaged in the Great Fire. Wren rebuilt the tower and steeple. The church was destroyed in the Second World War.*

74. *St Mary-le-Bow, rebuilt by Wren and modelled on the Basilica of Maxentius at Rome.*

Wren feared that, as costs mounted, there might be pressure either to scale down his designs or abort the project half-completed. He therefore realised the whole ground-plan simultaneously, layer by layer, rather than section by section, to circumvent this.

As a result it was not until 1697 that even a part of the building could actually be used for services. A supervising parliamentary committee took revenge by holding back half of Wren's fees so that by the time the work was finished the architect was years in arrears and had to petition the monarch for payment.

Wren's achievement was aesthetic, scientific and managerial. Artistically, it was a triumphant statement of the baroque. Less obviously, it was a triumph of engineering, its walls and pillars supporting a dome of 64,000 tons, equivalent in weight to the liner QE2. Wren also had the skill to select, motivate and control a team of craftsmen which included the English masons Strong and Kempster, the Dutch-born wood-carver Grinling Gibbons, the Danish sculptor Cibber and the French metal-worker, Tijou.

Contemporaries and posterity have saluted St Paul's as a masterpiece worthy of its creator. A sceptical Georgian wit observed that most people rather missed the point :

No thought arises of the life to come.
For, tho' superb, not solemn is the place,
The mind but wanders o'er the distant space,
Where, 'stead of thinking on their God, most men
Forget his presence to remember Wren.

By a nice touch of irony the rebuilding of public edifices was financed by a levy on coal. St Paul's alone accounted for about half of the total raised, costing some £750,000 – about enough to rebuild the entire navy; but as it was not completed until 1710 the burden was spread over almost half a century. Similarly the spires of most of Wren's fifty-one City churches were built a decade or more after the main body of the building, as the necessary cash was accumulated. Soaring above the homes and shops which hemmed them in as closely as in ancient days, Wren's intricate spires aptly symbolised the dynamism of a community which had literally been reborn from its own ashes. And, cleansed by fire, the City was never to be visited by plague again.

75. *St Michael Paternoster Royal, College Hill, rebuilt by Wren after the Great Fire. The 'Royal' is a corruption of La Reole in France, from where local vintners imported wine. Painted by James S. Ogilvy, 1910.*

Literary London

CRADLE AND MAGNET

No single city can, perhaps, claim to be the birthplace of English literature but the City can claim to have been its forcing-house. If neither Shakespeare, nor Johnson, nor Dickens were born in the City, they were all drawn to live in it. And Chaucer, Milton, Gray, and Keats were all City men by birth. Malory wrote the *Morte d'Arthur* while languishing in Newgate, and John Cleland composed *Fanny Hill: Memoirs of a Woman of Pleasure* while incarcerated in the Fleet. The Mermaid Tavern which once stood in Bread Street was the favoured haunt of Marlowe, Shakespeare, Donne, Beaumont, Fletcher and Drayton, members of a literary club founded by Sir Walter Ralegh, which met on the first Friday of the month. Keats, in his *Lines on the Mermaid Tavern* wondered whether the dead poets would have preferred Elysium or a reunion at the Mermaid. Charterhouse numbers among its pupils Lovelace, Addison, Steele, F.T. Palgrave (he of *The Golden Treasury*) and Thackeray – who unkindly referred to it in *Vanity Fair* as 'Slaughterhouse'. Those who have studied, resided or worked in the Temple include Ralegh, Evelyn and Cowper, the dramatists Beaumont, Webster, Congreve, Wycherley and Sheridan, the novelists Thomas Hughes (*Tom Brown's*

Schooldays), H. Rider-Haggard (*King Solomon's Mines*), John Galsworthy (*The Forsyte Saga*) and Leslie Stephen, founding editor of the monumental *Dictionary of National Biography*. Charles Lamb was born there and Oliver Goldsmith is buried there.

FOUNDING FATHER

Geoffrey Chaucer (?1343-1400), born in Vintry, the son of a vintner, doubtless used his knowledge of the family business to good purpose when he served as controller of customs in the port of London, just as he drew on the literally passing scene for the characters in his *Canterbury Tales* when he lived in chambers in the gatehouse at Aldgate between 1374 and 1386, composing *Troylus and Crysede* in his off-duty hours. Chaucer's use of the 'East Midland' dialect of English commonly used in the capital helped establish its claim to become the basis of 'Standard English'.

THE LANGUAGE OF FAITH

The church of St Dunstan in the West enjoys a triple literary distinction. William Tyndale (*c.*1494-1536), who made the first complete translation of the New Testament into English to be printed, was a preacher here in 1523-4, just before he fled into exile. His vigorous prose, which aimed to bring the Gospel "even to the boy that driveth the plough", gave English such familiar phrases as "the powers that be" and "fight the good fight" and provided 90% of the text of

76. Geoffrey Chaucer. Oil painting by an unknown artist.

77. William Tyndale, from Hollar's Heroologia, *1620.*

78. John Donne. Miniature by Isaac Oliver.

79. John Milton. After a miniature by Faithorne. John Aubrey noted that "he was so faire that they called him the Lady of Christ's College".

the King James Authorized Version of the Bible. The metaphysical poet John Donne (1571-1631), who was born in Bread Street, was rector here before his inspirational preaching elevated him to the post of Dean of St Paul's. Izaak Walton (1593-1683), ironmonger and author of *The Compleat Angler*, was a vestryman here and wrote biographies of Donne and other Anglican divines such as Richard Hooker and George Herbert.

John Milton (1608-74) was born in Bread Street 'at the Sign of the Spread Eagle', where his father worked as a scrivener and composer of music, was educated at St Paul's, and lived for a while in a house in the churchyard of St. Bride's. A fulsome tribute to the capital is found in Cowper's translation of one of Milton's earliest Latin poems:

Too blest abode! No loveliness we see
In all the earth, but it abounds in thee.

The mature Milton, Puritan pamphleteer, praised it as "a city of refuge, the mansion-house of liberty". After living elsewhere in and around London for most of his life, he passed the last decade of his life in Bunhill Row, where he composed *Paradise Regained* . He died from "gout struck in" and was buried beside his father in St Giles, Cripplegate.

Milton's near-contemporary John Bunyan (1628-88), who worshipped at the same St Giles as a child, spent most of his life in and around Bedford, where he wrote the *Pilgrim's Progress*, but he died in

lodgings at Snow Hill and lies buried in Bunhill Fields.

The youthful 'Cavalier Poet' Richard Lovelace (1618-57) ("I could not love thee, Dear, so much, Loved I not honour more.") died in extreme poverty in the garret of a house in Gunpowder Alley, off Fleet Street and is buried in St Bride's. Educated at Charterhouse, he had grown up the handsome, dashing heir to great estates in Kent and served with distinction at court and in the field only to fall victim to political machinations which brought him two terms in prison (hence, his "Stone walls do not a prison make...") – and a career which perished with the King he had so loyally served.

DANIEL DEFOE

The varied and colourful career of Daniel Defoe (1660-1731), born in Fore Street the son of a London butcher, included a spell as a hosiery merchant in Cornhill, spying, pamphleteering for both Tories and Whigs, journalism, travel-writing, and, he claimed, the making and losing of a dozen fortunes. The City provided Defoe with much material for a prolific literary output of some 560 books, journals and broadsides. The eponymous heroine of *Moll Flanders* is born in

80. Fleet Street, showing Temple Bar and, on the right, St Dunstan in the West church. Oil painting c.1750.

81. Daniel Defoe. Charles Lamb declared that "his fictions have all the air of true stories."

Newgate and Jack Sheppard, the popular thief whose exploits Defoe chronicled, notoriously escaped from the same prison repeatedly. Defoe knew it, quite literally, from the inside. *A Journal of the Plague Year*, though written more than half a century after the great visitation of 1665, remains an imaginative *tour de force*. Even when travelling far from the capital, Defoe remained constantly aware of its significance in the economic as well as the political life of the whole nation. The power of the London market in stimulating demand for specific products, from Newcastle coal to Norfolk turkeys, runs as a recurrent theme through his *Tour Through the Whole Island of Great Britain*. The continuing expansion of the capital which was the consequence of this dynamism was, however, no great blessing in his eyes:

It is the disaster of London, as to the beauty of its figure, that it is thus stretched out in buildings, just at the pleasure of every builder ... and as the convenience of the people directs ... and this has spread the face of it in a most straggling, confus'd manner, out of all shape, incompact and unequal; neither long nor broad, round nor square ... whither will this monstrous city then extend?"

Defoe died, uncharacterisically "of lethargy", in lodgings in Ropemaker's Alley (now Street), Moorfields and was buried in Bunhill Fields, 'the Dissenter's Westminster Abbey'.

NO LOVERS OF LONDON

Alexander Pope (1688-1744) was born in Plough Court, off Lombard Street but spent most of his life outside the City, noting tartly in a youthful satire:

Yes; thank my stars! as early as I knew
This Town, I had the sense to hate it too.

In 1715 he published an equally acerbic *Farewell to London*:

Dear, damn'd, distracting Town, farewell!
Thy fools no more I'll tease:
This Year in Peace, ye Critics, dwell,
Ye Harlots, sleep at Ease!

The passage of a quarter of a century scarcely moderated Pope's bile and even when ostensibly composing a commentary on the *Epistles* of Horace he could not forbear a side-swipe at the City:

There, London's voice " 'Get money still!
And then let virtue follow if she will.'

Thomas Gray (1716-71), author of the much anthologized *Elegy in a Country Churchyard*, took a similarly baleful attitude towards his birthplace, stigmatising it wearily as "That tiresome dull place! where all people under thirty find so much amusement". Born in Cornhill, the son of a scrivener and a milliner, Gray passed most of his life at Cambridge, his alma mater.

JOHNSON AND HIS CIRCLE

Samuel Johnson (1709-84) walked from his native Lichfield to London in 1737 and lived for most of the rest of his life in the courts and alleys off Fleet Street.

A quarter of a century after his arrival Johnson could therefore admonish his new young friend James Boswell with an authority born of experience that:

Sir, if you wish to have a just notion of the magnitude of this city, you must not be satisfied with its great streets and squares, but must survey the innumerable little lanes and courts. It is not in the showy evolution of buildings, but in the multiplicity of human habitations which are crowded together, that the wonderful immensity of London consists.

Johnson's satirical poem *London* appeared the year after his arrival and pungently records the very diverse hazards of metropolitan life:

Here malice, rapine, accident conspire,
And now a rabble rages, now a fire;
Their ambush here relentless ruffians lay,
And here the fell attorney prowls for prey;
Here falling houses thunder on your head
And here a female atheist talks you dead.

Johnson lived on the edge of debt during his early years in London, scribbling frantically against constant deadlines, hence his famous *Dictionary* definition of what would nowadays be called hack work –

82. Alexander Pope. Pencil drawing by Jonathan Richardson.

83. Samuel Johnson, from the painting by Joshua Reynolds.

84. Dr Johnson's House in Gough Square, off Fleet Street, where he lived from 1748 to 1758. It is now open to the public.

"Grub Street. Originally the name of a street near Moorfields in London, much inhabited by writers of small histories, dictionaries and temporary poems, whence any mean production is called *grubstreet*." In the nineteenth century this notorious name was replaced, apparently without ironic or iconic intention, by the designation Milton Street .

Both name and thoroughfare disappeared entirely as casualties of re-development in the 1960s.

Knowing poverty well, Johnson relished both comfort and company and it was probably the now-vanished Mitre in Fleet Street which provoked his genial observation that "there is nothing that has yet been contrived by man, by which so much happiness is produced as by a good tavern or inn."

Johnson recognised the *completeness* of London. One of his most famous sayings, so rarely quoted in full, makes this point convincingly. When Boswell suggested that, if he were to live in London permanently, he would lose "the exquisite zest with which I relished it in occasional visits", Johnson replied magisterially:

Why, Sir, you find no man, at all intellectual, who is willing to leave London. No, Sir, when a man is tired of London, he is tired of life; for there is in London all that life can afford.

Johnson's friend Oliver Goldsmith (1730-74) lodged

85. Oliver Goldsmith.

between 1760 and 1762 in Wine Office Court where he ran up rent arrears of £36, which his landlady attempted to extort from him by seizing all his clothes. Johnson rescued the spendthrift Irishman by selling for sixty guineas the manuscript of a novel he had been working on while living there. *The Vicar of Wakefield* appeared in print four years later.

THE 'COCKNEY SCHOOL'

Charles Lamb (1775-1834) was born in Crown Office Row in the Temple and educated at Christ's Hospital, where he formed an enduring friendship with Coleridge, whom in later years he referred to as "an archangel slightly damaged" and to whom he dedicated his *Essays of Elia*. For almost his entire adult existence Lamb worked at the East India House, retiring to north London only for the last decade of his life. His love of the City was profound and he delighted in the people as much as the place, assuring readers of the *Morning Post* that "The passion for crowds is nowhere feasted so full as in London. The man must have a rare recipe for melancholy who can be dull in Fleet Street." In a letter to Wordsworth that was both a confession and a challenge Lamb wrote:

"My attachments are all local, purely local. I have no passion ... to groves and valleys. The rooms where I was born ... streets, squares, where I have sunned myself, my old school – these are my mistresses. Have I not enough, without your mountains?"

86. Charles Lamb. "May my last breath be drawn through a pipe and exhaled in a pun," he declared.

Leigh Hunt (1784-1859) was another Christ's Hospital boy and became part of Lamb's circle, publishing Lamb's essays on Shakespeare and Hogarth in his journal, the *Reflector*. A fine essayist but indifferently successful as a dramatist, Hunt was also gifted as a literary talent-spotter and was an early and committed supporter of Keats.

John Keats (1795-1821) was born the son of the manager of a livery stable in Moorfields and as a young man lodged with his brother at 76 Cheapside. After studying at Guy's Hospital, he was accepted by the Society of Apothecaries as a qualified member of that profession. In 1817 his first volume of poems was savaged by a review in the Edinburgh-based *Blackwood's Magazine*, which vilified him as the leader of a 'Cockney School' of versifiers and bade him stick to pills and potions. Since his early death Keats' reputation has remained high. Tennyson considered him the greatest poet of his century and T.S. Eliot considered his posthumously published letters to be "the most notable and most important ever written by any English poet."

Thomas Love Peacock (1785-1866) was the son of a London glass merchant but inherited just enough to live on while establishing a literary reputation as a poet and satirist before entering the service of the East India Company in 1819. The standard Peacock novel revolves around the extravagant conversations of absurd eccentrics in an imaginary country house (viz. *Headlong Hall* (1816), *Nightmare Abbey* (1818), *Crotchet Castle* (1831) but he did draw on his knowledge of the

87. John Keats. From the painting by William Hilton. Keats recorded of himself, "I think I shall be among the English Poets after my death."

City to lampoon the futile dogmas of economists and skullduggery of bankers in *The Paper Money Lyrics* (1837) – just as he was succeeding the eminent James Mill in occupying the very senior post of Examiner.

Thomas Hood (1799-1845) was born in Poultry, the son of a bookseller, and celebrated his birthplace in verse:

I remember, I remember,
The house where I was born,
The little window where the sun
Came peeping in at morn.

Hood worked as assistant editor on the brilliant but short-lived *London Magazine* which was founded in opposition to the partisan *Blackwood's* and published work by that 'Cockney School' which included Hunt and Hazlitt as well as Lamb and Keats. An inspired punster, Hood aspired to be a savage critic of his times but lacked edge in his satires, leading Lamb to dismiss him genially as "our half-Hogarth".

The literary career of Charles Dickens (1812-70) may be said to have begun in Johnson's Court, off Fleet Street, when "stealthily one evening at twilight with fear and trembling" he dropped a manuscript through the letter-box of the offices of the *Monthly Magazine*. The published item became part of his first work *Sketches by Boz*.

88. *(Top left)* *William Harrison Ainsworth.*

89. *(Top right)* *Thomas Love Peacock.*

90. *(Bottom right)* *Thomas Hood.*

TAIL-ENDERS

Dickens' friend, the historical novelist Harrison Ainsworth (1805-82), wrote most of *The Tower of London* while living at the Sussex Hotel in Bouverie Street in 1840 and celebrated its completion by giving a slap-up dinner there. Contributors to *Punch* dined regularly at No. 10 in the same street in that decade. Mark Lemon, the founding editor and another friend of Dickens, was the first to publish one of Hood's most famous (and gloomy) works *The Song of the Shirt*, an indictment of female exploitation in the garment industry.

As the City ceased to be a place of residence its contribution to literature became increasingly indirect, limited to the productions of those who worked rather than lived there. Kenneth Grahame (1859-1932) worked at the Bank of England from 1898 until 1908 when *The Wind in the Willows* was published to an initially muted reception. T.S. Eliot (1888-1965) worked at Lloyd's Bank in Cornhill and Lombard Street. Grateful though he was to escape schoolmastering, the zombie-like state of the commuters he depicted plodding up King William Street in *The Waste Land* suggests that his exodus to publishing in Bloomsbury was just as gratefully embraced.

Streets of Ink

BOOKS AND BOOKSELLERS

William Caxton established England's first printing press in the shadow of Westminster Abbey. After his death his assistant and successor, Wynkyn de Worde (Wynandus Van Woerden), brought it to Fleet Street around 1500 and printed almost eight hundred works there before his death in 1535. In 1502 Richard Pynson joined de Worde in Fleet Street and became printer to the Crown in 1508. His successor in that post, Thomas Berthelet of Blackfriars, imported Italian craftsmen to produce England's first gilt-tooled bindings. A complete edition of the works of Sir Thomas More was eventually produced by yet another Fleet Street printer, his nephew William Rastell.

The streets and lanes around the Cathedral already had a long association with the book trade. A (female) bookbinder is recorded as living in Fleet Street as early as 1311. In 1557 the Stationers' Company received a royal charter which in effect gave it control of the publishing industry. Until 1911 all new titles had to be registered at Stationers' Hall and the present Livery is still completely drawn from the trade. To the normal financial risks inherent in any business, publishing for centuries added legal and political ones. Stow records that one William Carter, having been imprisoned several times for printing "naughty papysticall books", persisted in this course until, in 1584, he was finally drawn from Newgate to Tyburn to be hanged, drawn and quartered. In 1586 the number of presses was limited by law.

St Paul's Churchyard, Carter Lane, Paternoster Row and Little Britain housed the core of the publishing industry in Britain from the sixteenth century until it was blitzed out in 1940. Longman's, Nelson's and Hutchinson's then relocated elsewhere. But three major publishers – Oxford University Press, Hodder and Routledge – were still there in the 1960s.

Distinctions between printer, publisher and bookseller emerged only gradually. Apart from the main clusters of booksellers around St Paul's Churchyard and in Little Britain (where Ben Franklin lodged when he was working as a printer in the 1720s), another group of rather down-market ones were to be found on London Bridge, no doubt relying on the passing trade of travellers newly arrived in the city. Although the fashionable Strand and Pall Mall eventually emerged as the preferred locations for up-market outlets for books and prints, in the early nineteenth century Lackington's 'Temple of the Muses' in Finsbury Square was still the largest bookshop in London. Holywell Street, from which all sign of its past connection has now vanished, was once Booksellers' Row but Farringdon Road, until recently, still had a much-diminished version of its once celebrated open-air market for secondhand titles.

91. Stationers' Company Hall (1770).

92. *'A Windy day in St Paul's Churchyard', showing a printseller in the background. Drawing by Robert Dighton.*

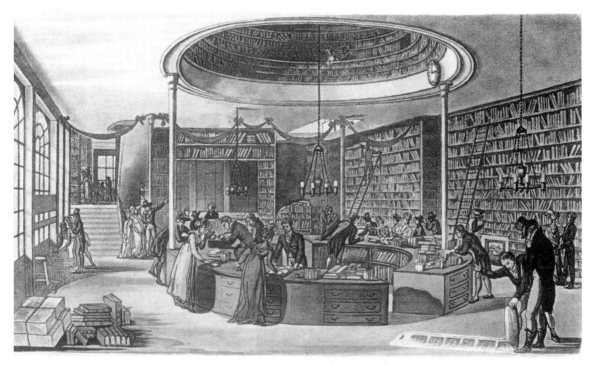

93. *James Lackington's Temple of the Muses in Finsbury Square.*

94. *Benjamin Franklin, from the painting by M. Chamberlin.*

CITY CLASSICS

City firms are among the most famous in publishing history and many classic works of English literature were first published within the City's boundaries. Many of the earliest printed versions of Shakespeare's works, including *Hamlet* and the *Sonnets*, originated in St Paul's Churchyard. The First Folio of his complete works was published in 1623 at Barbican, priced one pound. Milton's *Paradise Lost* was first sold in Little Britain, where *The Spectator* was also first printed in 1711.

Robinson Crusoe, the mysteriously anonymous *Letters of Junius* which savaged the Grafton and North ministries between 1769 and 1772, and the 1798 *Lyrical Ballads* of Wordsworth and Coleridge, which revolutionised English poetry, were all published in Paternoster Row. Boswell's *Life of Samuel Johnson* was published by Dilly Brothers of Poultry, where Johnson had been tricked into dining with John Wilkes – and unexpectedly succumbed to the notorious rake's charm and vivacity. Dilly Brothers were also the earliest publishers to specialise in Americana. John Murray established himself at 32 Fleet Street until his success with Byron's *Don Juan* enabled him to move west to Albemarle Street. Another Scottish firm, Macmillan's, established itself in Aldersgate Street in 1843. In 1848 the offices of Smith, Elder at 65 Cornhill

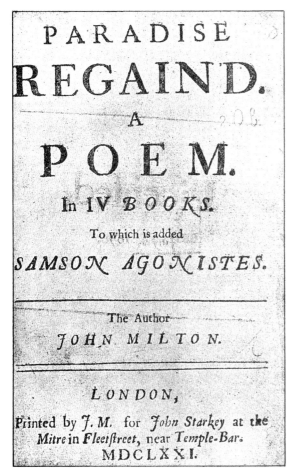

95. Title page of the first edition of Paradise Regained, *1671. Printed at The Mitre in Fleet Street.*

96. Samuel Richardson; oil painting by Jospeh Highmore.

Richardson's near-contemporary John Newbery (1713-67) was the inventor of children's publishing. *Mother Goose* and *Goody Two Shoes* were among his titles and the Newbery Prize, named in his honour, has become the most prestigious award conferred by American librarians in recognition of outstanding works of children's literature.

THE FOURTH ESTATE

Fleet Street's association with newspapers and journals dates back to the translations of foreign newsletters which were circulated among subscribers in the seventeeth century. England's first regular daily general interest paper, the *Daily Courant*, was published in 1702 "next to the King's Arms tavern by Fleet Bridge." In 1708 Defoe described the *Daily Courant* as being run by a club of twenty booksellers and having a circulation of 800. This journal lasted thirty-three years and was joined by the *Daily Post* (1719-46) and *Daily Journal* (1721-37). The *Gentleman's Magazine* appeared first in Red Lion Court in 1731 and managed to survive until 1907.

The Times was established in Printing House Square in 1785. Its extraordinary position in Britain's national life was established within a generation. By 1823 William Hazlitt, himself a former employee, could hail it as:

were the scene of a celebrated literary encounter when the publisher and his most important author, Thackeray, were astonished to discover at their first meeting that the promising young authors Currer and Acton Bell were in fact Charlotte and Anne Bronte.

Samuel Richardson (1689-1761) ran a highly successful business in Salisbury Court, printing everything from advertising flyers to the Tory *True Briton* and ultimately the journals of the House of Commons. Richardson's *Pamela* (1741) and *Clarissa* (1747) are regarded as landmarks in the history of the novel and achieved huge popularity in Europe. In his *Dictionary* Johnson quoted from *Clarissa* 97 times, almost double the number from any other single work. In 1754-5 Richardson served as Master of the Stationers' Company and the year after was consulted by Oxford University on the reform of its press.

... the greatest engine of temporary opinion in the world ... the witness of the British metropolis: the mouthpiece, oracle and echo of the Stock Exchange, the origin of the mercantile interest ... It takes up no falling cause; fights no uphill battle; advocates no great principle ... It is ever stronger upon the stronger side.

The main market rival to *The Times* was the *Morning Advertiser*. Founded in 1815, it was the first daily to be published in Fleet Street itself, at No. 127, until 1929.

What *The Times* and *Morning Advertiser* were to the Establishment, the *Political Register* edited by William Cobbett (1763-1835) was to its opponents. Born in Westminster in 1802, but printed by T.C. Hansard of Peterborough Court ("the very best printer in London") it was published mostly from 183 Fleet Street and later from Bolt Court. Its 4,000 a week circulation of 1805 had risen to over 60,000 by 1816, according to philosopher Jeremy Bentham. Less precisely Hazlitt said it sold "like pancakes, hot and hot" The *Political*

97. *(Above) Edward Cave, publisher of* The Gentleman's Magazine. *From a painting by F. Kyte, 1740.*

98. *(Below) Masthead of an early copy of* The Times, *still displaying its first title,* The Daily Universal Register.

99. *(Top right) Masthead of the first* Gentleman's Magazine *in 1731, showing St John's Gate, where it was printed.*

100. Printing House Square and the offices of The Times, *1870.*

Register set a new trend for racy, direct writing in the American style. By promoting its proprietor's general opinions, rather than carrying news as such, it evaded the onerous Stamp Tax and could be published at a cover price of twopence, which put it within the reach of reform-minded labourers, clubbing together in groups to buy it and read it aloud.

PRINT FOR THE PEOPLE

Publisher Charles Knight (1791-1873) was the first to produce non-political periodicals and books intended for the working-classes. Working through his Fleet Street-based Society for the Diffusion of Useful Knowledge, he churned out such titles as *The Penny Magazine*, *The Penny Cyclopaedia* and *The Library of Useful Knowledge*, as well as illustrated histories of London and England and an illustrated edition of Shakespeare. His autobiographical *Passages of a Working Life* (1864-5) contains much valuable information about the publishing trade in his day.

Tiny Crane Court gave birth to two famous publications – *Punch* founded at No. 9 in 1841 and the *Illustrated London News* founded at No. 10 the following year. Edward Lloyd's *Lloyd's Weekly Newspaper*, also founded in 1842, was the first to reach a world record circulation of a million, a record equalled by the *News of the World*, which dates from 1843. The *Daily News*, established in 1846, had Dickens as its first editor – for twenty days. He never tried editing a daily again but the redoubtable bluestocking Harriet Martineau (1802-76), despite delicate health and profound deafness, proved of sterner stuff, contributing

101. Charles Knight; industrious and influential, he both created and profited from the artisan intellectual.

102. Waiting for copies of the Illustrated London News *in the Strand.*

no less than 1,600 leaders over the years. The paper itself survived until 1930, when it sold its site to the *Daily Express* and merged with the *Daily Chronicle*, which had been founded in Salisbury Square in 1869, to form the *News Chronicle*.

By 1846 thirty-five papers and periodicals were being published in Fleet Street, including three dailies. The abolition of advertisement duty, Stamp Duty and paper duty in 1853, 1855 and 1861 effectively deregulated the press and led to such a proliferation of new titles that by 1891 Fleet Street was home to over three hundred, including eleven dailies.

NEWSPAPER PEOPLE

In 1855 *The Daily Telegraph* opened a new chapter in newspaper history as London's first morning paper to be sold for just one penny. Its most famous writer, was the pugnacious, dandyish, alcoholic George Augustus Sala (1828-95) whose bulbous nose was often said to be Fleet Street's most prominent landmark. Having served as Dickens' correspondent in the Crimean War, he was a welcome if trying addition to the staff of the *Daily Telegraph*, quite capable of turning out a leader on anything from the price of fish to court intrigues in St Petersburg. Other outstanding Fleet Street characters included the sensationalist W.T. Stead (1849-1912) – "muckraker for God" – who used the *Pall Mall Gazette* to run an exposé of child prostitution in London and his contemporary, the Irish Nationalist MP T.P. O'Connor (1848-1929), who served continuously in the Commons for over forty years. The influential despatches sent from the Crimea to *The Times* by William Howard Russell (1820-1907), criticising the mismanagement of the war, enhanced the role and romantic profile of the daring foreign correspondent. Russell was knighted in 1895, a singular tribute to the rising status of the journalist.

103. *George Augustus Sala, by Ape in* Vanity Fair.

104. *Alfred Harmsworth, by Spy, 1895. 'He aspired to power instead of influence, and as a result forfeited both.' (A.J.P. Taylor.)*

The link between Fleet Street and the wider world was symbolised and reinforced by the decision of Thomas Cook's travel agency to establish their head-quarters there in 1873. Such was the glamour of Fleet Street and its denizens that few can have mistaken what journalist Philip Gibb (1877-1962) was referring to when he entitled his account of it *The Street of Adventure* (1909).

The increasing volume and variety of publications flooding out of Fleet Street at last compelled the construction of purpose-built printing-works. The first was James Moye's Temple Printing Office, which opened at the junction of Bouverie Street and Tudor Street in 1826. Half a century later it would be com-pletely dwarfed by the massive La Belle Sauvage printing works in Fleet Lane, just east of Ludgate Circus, opened by Cassell, Petter and Galpin in 1875.

To cope with the surging tide of its traffic, Fleet Street was much widened between 1880 and 1914, with almost the whole of its south side east of the Temple being aligned back. Farringdon Street was also widened and Ludgate Circus laid out.

105. *The Daily Telegraph building, Fleet Street, in the 1930s.*

NORTHCLIFFE'S 'NEW JOURNALISM'

The Street's commanding position in the field of mass-communications was further strengthened by the advent of Alfred Harmsworth (1865-1922) who introduced such American-style innovations as ban-ner-headlines, photographic illustrations, cheque-book journalism and publicity stunts. This 'New Jour-nalism' was aimed at the products of the new elemen-tary schools, whose grasp of literacy and public af-fairs were assumed to be as shaky as their attention-span was short. Its emergence also coincided with the general adoption of two other American innovations – the linotype machine and the telephone – which greatly diminished the gap between the occurrence of an event and its reportage in print, thus providing a further stimulus to sensationalism. Having acquired

106. The Daily Express building, Fleet Street, in the 1930s.

control of the *Evening News* in 1894, Harmsworth founded the *Daily Mail* in 1896, housing it in the splendour of Carmelite House (built 1897-9). Avowedly cheap and cheerful – "a penny newspaper for a ha'penny" – the *Mail* pioneered the idea of a woman's page but was dismissed by its rivals as being "written by office-boys for office-boys". Its success encouraged Harmsworth to establish the *Daily Mirror* in

1903 as an even more populist running-mate. Elevated to the peerage in 1905 as Lord Northcliffe he took over *The Times* itself and boosted its circulation from 38,000 to 318,000. During the Great War Northcliffe served as the nation's director of propaganda. He died a Viscount and is commemorated by a memorial, designed by Lutyens, outside St Dunstan in the West.

The Sound of Music

ORGANIZING HARMONY
The lunchtime concerts staged in so many City churches, which come as such an unexpected delight to so many visitors, perpetuate a musical tradition stretching back to the Middle Ages. The Musicians' Company published ordinances regulating members as early as 1350 and received its royal charter of incorporation in 1500.

In 1905 the Company took the lead in reviving the seventeenth-century tradition of a concert to celebrate St Cecilia's Day, which falls on 22 November. Ranking fiftieth in precedence, the Company still concerns itself with professional standards through awards to performers and composers.

Other important City-based initiatives which have shaped the development of the musical profession include the foundation of the Guildhall School of Music by the City Corporation in 1880 and the establishment of the London Symphony Orchestra, the capital's oldest, in 1904. In the 1920s the City also provided the setting for the recording of two of the first-ever million-seller popular classics – Mendelssohn's *Hear My Prayer*, recorded by the Temple choir and Master Ernest Luff's *O, for the Wings of a Dove*, recorded at the City Temple.

PROFESSIONAL POSITIONS
From Tudor times onwards the incorporation of organ music into Christian worship created posts for professional musicians which were fairly permanent and occasionally prominent, if usually poorly paid. The great Thomas Tallis (1505-85) 'father of English church music', was the organist of St Mary-at-Hill. A

lifelong servant of the Crown, Tallis undoubtedly benefited from the fact that Elizabeth I, like her father, was an accomplished musician. In 1575 the Queen granted him, jointly with William Byrd (1543-1623), the monopoly of importing and printing music and music paper in England. In the following generation Thomas Morley (1557-1603), organist at St Paul's, edited *The Triumphs of Oriana*, which has been hailed as "probably the greatest collection of madrigals ever compiled." His other, more down to earth, publishing accomplishment was a *Plaine and Easie Introduction to Practicall Musicke*. Another St Paul's organist, Jeremiah Clarke (1674-1707) was the composer of the *Trumpet Voluntary* frequently attributed to Purcell. Tragically, Clarke committed suicide after being spurned in love.

SPECIAL ST PAUL'S
The sheer size and status of St Paul's has guaranteed it a special place in the City's musical history. The monumental organ built for Wren's church by Bernard Schmidt was famously favoured by both Handel, who would play for hours on summer evenings, stripped to the waist, and, a century later, by Mendelssohn.

St Paul's was kind to Handel. Arriving in England in 1712, he marked the conclusion of the long War of Spanish Succession in 1713 by composing a celebratory *Te Deum* for the thanksgiving service held in the cathedral. Queen Anne was so delighted with it that she awarded him a royal pension of £200 a year. St Paul's organist John Goss (1800-80), composer of *Praise, my Soul, the King of Heaven*, was a less happy recipient of royal satisfaction. His playing at the thanksgiving service for the recovery of the Prince of Wales from typhoid in 1871 so pleased Queen Victoria that she bestowed a knighthood on him; but this

107. Thomas Tallis.

108. William Byrd.

109. *Street musician with large barrel organ; from the* Illustrated London News *19 Dec 1846).*

did nothing for him financially and he grumbled thereafter that he was "the only knight in Brixton".

PARISH CHURCHES AND STREET SINGERS

Two other City churches merit special mention for their contributions to English musical history.

St Michael's Cornhill possesses a Renatus Harris organ, dating from 1684, which was played by Purcell. In 1864 the organist of St Michael's, R.D. Limpus, took the initiative in founding the Royal College of Organists which, since 1991 has returned to the City and now has its headquarters at St Andrew's, Holborn. One of Limpus's successors, Harold Darke (1888-1966), served St Michael's for over fifty years and is memorialized by his much-loved carol *In the Bleak Midwinter.*

The church of the Holy Sepulchre in Newgate Street also possessed a Harris organ from 1677 until 1932. This was also played by Handel and Mendelssohn, but perhaps more significantly, was the organ on which Henry Wood (1869-1944), founder of the Proms, learned to play. The tomb containing his ashes dominates the chapel of St Cecilia, which was specifically dedicated as the Musicians' Chapel in 1955. Stained-glass windows honour the organist John Ireland (1879-1962) and the famed opera singer Dame Nellie Melba (1861-1931) in her roles as Mimi and Desdemona.

Street musicians were a permanent feature of City life from medieval times until the beginning of the present century. The musicality of vendors hawking their wares inspired Orlando Gibbons' (1583-1625) *Cries of London*, while street ballads, celebrating love and low life, provide much of the libretto for Gay's *Beggar's Opera* (1728).

Scientific Minds

The City may have always been more a place of commerce than of learning, and its learning may usually have been of a severely practical kind, but its contributions to the progress of science, technology and medicine have been considerable.

ASTROLABES, ELECTRICITY AND BLOOD

Geoffrey Chaucer was not only an accomplished man of letters but also a keen astronomer and the author of a standard treatise on the astrolabe. And it was one H. Billingsley, proudly styling himself 'Citizen of London', who was responsible, in 1570, for the first printed translation of Euclid's *Geometry* in English. Citizen Billingsley became successively Sheriff, Lord Mayor and MP.

The pioneering work on electricity, *De magnete*, written by William Gilbert (1540-1603) of Colchester, the queen's physician, was printed in London in 1600.

And, just as Gilbert discovered that the earth was a great magnet, so Harvey discovered that the heart was a tireless pump. William Harvey (1578-1657), who was appointed to the staff of St Bartholomew's Hospital in 1609 and became physician to James I in 1618, published his epochal account of the circulation of the blood, *Exercitatio de Moto Cordis et Sanguinis* in 1628. He had, however, been propagating his revolutionary theory since 1616 in his lectures at the College of Physicians in Knightrider Street.

TEACHING AND LEARNING

That great Tudor tycoon Sir Thomas Gresham (?1519-79) left money in his will to found Gresham College to deliver free public instruction in Divinity, Law, Rhetoric and Music – and also in Physics, Geometry and Astronomy. The lectures were initially given at his former house in Broad Street. The first professional appointment taken up by Christopher Wren (1632-1723), after graduating from Oxford, was to become Professor of Astronomy at Gresham College, aged twenty-five. Wren may have become a workaholic architect of genius, but he still claimed to have made fifty-three "inventions and discoveries" and remained an active member of the Royal Society, like those other prominent City figures, diarist Samuel Pepys (1633-1703) and City Surveyor, Robert Hooke (1635-1703).

The Royal Society, Europe's oldest learned institution devoted to science, evolved from informal weekly meetings first held at "the Bull's Head tavern in Cheapside till it grew too big for a club, and so they came to Gresham College parlour." The Society continued to meet at the College until 1710, when it

110. *William Harvey.* "....*had he been stiffe, starchl und retired, as other formall Doctors are, he had known no more than they. From the meanest person, in some way, or other, the learnedst man may learn something.*" (*John Aubrey,* Brief Lives.)

moved to Crane Court, off Fleet Street, where it stayed until 1780. The learned papers considered by the Society in its early days were, to say the least, wide-ranging in scope, encompassing both speculative theory (*On the Transmutation of Water into Maggots*) and severe practicality (*An Easy Way of Taking a Vomit*).

Gresham's house was finally pulled down in 1768 but the lectures continued, fittingly being given in a room above the Royal Exchange, Gresham's great creation. In 1843 the College moved to purpose-built accommodation in Gresham Street, a fortuitous relocation which spared it the ravages of the fire which consumed the Exchange the following year. The lectures continue today under the trusteeship of the City and the Mercers' Company and with the practical co-operation of City University.

In 1805 the London Institution was founded "for the Advancement of Literature and the Diffusion of Useful Knowledge". For the first dozen years of its existence its meetings were held in Sir Robert Clayton's house in Old Jewry. In 1819 it moved into a handsome neo-classical building on the north side of Finsbury Circus.

In 1820 its programme of lectures included courses

111. *Gresham College*

112. *The Royal College of Physicians in Warwick Lane, a building designed by Christopher Wren and Robert Hooke. The College moved to Trafalgar Square in 1825, and to their present building in Regent's Park in 1964.*

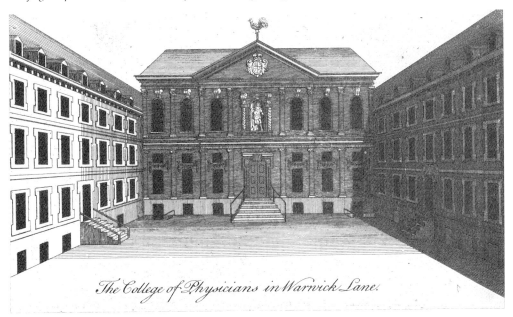

The College of Physicians in Warwick Lane.

113. *A meeting of members at the Royal College of Physicians in Warwick Lane, depicted by Pugin and Rowlandson.*

on botany, chemistry, 'Experimental Philosophy' ('Hydraulics, Mechanics, Optics, and the use of Steam Engines') and 'Natural Philosophy' ('viz. Astronomy, Optics, Hydrostatics and Mechanics; to be illustrated by Experiments.'), the latter given gratis by the great pioneer of popular education for 'mechanics', George Birkbeck.

The building was finally demolished in 1936.

SCIENTIFIC INSTRUMENTS

As Britain's largest port London was naturally a major centre for the manufacture of navigational aids and consequently of other types of scientific instruments such as microscopes, barometers and chronometers. One of the most eminent practitioners was Thomas Tompion (1639-1713), 'father of English watchmaking', whose workshop stood at the corner of Fleet Street and Whitefriars Street. In 1675 Tompion collaborated with Robert Hooke to make one of the first English watches with a balance spring. In 1695 he was granted a patent for the cylinder escapement he devised. Tompion's standing in his field can be judged from the fact that he was not only clockmaker to the newly-founded Royal Observatory at Greenwich and official supplier of barometers and sundials to William III but also honoured with burial in the nave of Westminster Abbey.

Edward Troughton (1753-1835), a maker of scientific instruments and another Fleet Street resident, was the co-founder of the Royal Astronomical Society in 1820 and a Fellow of the Royal Society. His firm was the official supplier of surveying instruments to the Ordnance Survey and East India Company. The first Secretary of the Royal Astronomical Society was Francis Baily (1774-1844), a retired City financier, whose interests included not only astronomy but also history and actuarial theory.

Pleasures of the City

So long as the City retained a substantial residential population it remained a place for leisure and amusement as well as work. William FitzStephen, writing around 1180, described the martial and athletic pursuits of young apprentices larking about on the open land north of the City walls but he also mentions acrobats whose feats (balancing on sword-points, stilt-walking with a jug of water on the head) clearly imply professional skills. Five hundred years later such cultured men as Pepys and Evelyn by no means thought themselves superior to the appeal of rope-dancers, fire-eaters, bearded women and the novelty of Punch and Judy puppet shows.

COMIC AND CURIOUS

Curiosities – horrific, historic and fantastic – were the stock-in-trade of Mrs Salmon's waxworks which filled six rooms at St Martin's le Grand before moving to Fleet Street in 1711. Hogarth and Boswell were both patrons and it survived well into Victorian times. The East India Company Museum in Leadenhall Street, otherwise known as the 'Oriental Repository', displayed a collection of authentic curiosities, ranging from Buddhist statuary to musical instruments donated by the Company's officials. Pride of place was occupied by 'Tippoo's Tiger', an ingenious model of a tiger savaging a sepoy, complete with sound-effects from an organ mounted inside. Captured at the fall of Seringapatam, it went on show in 1808, was seen by Keats and, after the demise of the East India Company in 1858, passed to the Victoria & Albert Museum where it can still be seen.

FROST FAIRS

Very occasionally the Thames itself became a place of amusement, when the sluggish tide of the river, impeded by the piers supporting London Bridge, froze solid during extended periods of severe weather. In the winter of 1564-5 archers and dancers took to the ice. In 1683-4, when the freeze lasted right through December and January, booths lined a 'street' which stretched from Temple to Southwark; in one of them Charles II had his name printed as a souvenir on a piece of Dutch quarto paper. Other 'Frost Fairs' were held in 1715-16, 1739-40, 1788-89 and 1813-14, after which the reconstruction of old London Bridge so speeded the flow of the Thames that it never again froze sufficiently well to enable further such fairs to be held.

BARTHOLOMEW FAIR

The City's regular fair was Bartholomew Fair, held at Smithfield since 1133 and so named because its tolls went to support Bart's Hospital. Rahere, its founder, is said to have performed juggling tricks during the festivities but it had a serious side as well, being the biggest cloth fair in the country – hence Cloth Fair, which runs off Smithfield, adjacent to St Bartholomew-the-Great. Traditionally, the proceedings were opened by the Lord Mayor himself, ceremonially cutting a piece of cloth – a ritual later generally extended to hospitals, bridges etc to mark their formal inauguration.

In 1445 the City Corporation, which organised a simultaneous cattle fair, settled a long-standing dispute over tolls so that Priory and Corporation became

114. Mrs Salmon's Waxworks on the north side of Fleet Street, after a drawing by J.T. Smith. Mrs Salmon, who had a pronounced taste for the sensational, lived till the age of 90 and only on her death did control of her enterprise change hands. By 1795 it was on the south side of Fleet Street, on the corner with Inner Temple Lane.

115. *The Great Frost Fair on the Thames 1683/4. At the bottom of the steps on the left watermen – unemployed because of the freeze-up – offer to 'help' visitors across the slushy, slippery surface of the ice in return for a consideration. Notice the line of tented booths and the horse-drawn carriages. At the right an ice-yacht is being manoeuvred into position for a run.*

joint Lords of the Fair. The Corporation took over sole control in 1604. By then, as Jonson's play *Bartholomew Fair* (1614) suggests, entertainment had become far more important than economics, and it attracted far more bawds, bullies and balladeers than sober-sided merchants. The Fair continued to flourish and gained

a high reputation for the quality of its theatrical presentations, which included Gay's *The Beggar's Opera*. By Victorian times, however, it was seen as an encouragement to public disorder and immorality and was closed down by the Corporation in 1855.

116. Bartholomew Fair, depicted by Pugin and Rowlandson in the Microcosm of London *(1808). It notes of the crowd: 'To be pleased in their own way, is the object of all.'*

THEATRES

Although the first purpose-built theatres were strategically built outside the City's jurisdiction, at Shoreditch and Bankside, these disreputable entertainments soon attempted to establish themselves even closer to their potential audiences.

The frater of the former Blackfriars monastery was used as a playhouse between 1578 and 1582 and more successfully after 1597, when it was initially used by a juvenile troupe, the 'Children of the Chapel Royal', and a decade later was taken over by an actor-impresario consortium headed by Burbage and Shakespeare.

The Great Hall of the nearby Whitefriars monastery was similarly used, on an occasional basis, for some thirty years. The playhouse at Salisbury Court, off Fleet Street, was purpose-built in 1629 and like the other London theatres, closed down by the Puritans in 1642. Smashed up by Cromwellian soldiers in 1649, it nevertheless re-opened at the Restoration. Pepys went there for the premiere of *Tis a pitty she's a Whore*, which he thought "a simple play and ill acted." The playhouse disappeared in the Great Fire of 1666.

Its replacement was the Duke's Theatre, in Dorset Gardens, a magnificent building by Wren, which opened in 1671 with a production of Dryden's *Sir Martin Mar-All*. A year later, when Drury Lane Theatre burned down, the Duke's Theatre became the only theatre in London and for the next few years was at its peak. However, in 1682 the Duke's Company, one of the only two permitted to perform in London, merged with that at Drury Lane and left Dorset Gardens. The theatre-world and its followers inexorably went further west and in 1720 the Duke's Theatre (by then called the Queen's) was demolished and a timber yard took its place.

From Elkannah Settles

Empress of Morocco

117. The Duke's Theatre in Dorset Gardens, off Fleet Street.

Places of Learning

England's most ancient universities, significantly, were located not in the capital, with its concentration of noise, dirt and distractions, but a couple of days' ride away. The City has ever been a place for doers, rather than thinkers, a place where the acute minds of lawyers, journalists and entrepreneurs have been focused on practical problems, rather than abstract speculations. In Tudor times, however, the Temple certainly rivalled Oxford and Cambridge as a seat of learning, not simply for training professional lawyers but also as a sort of finishing school for the gentry, most of whom needed a smattering of legal knowledge to serve on the bench as JPs or dispute wills with their relatives or boundaries with their neighbours.

SCHOOLS

The City has, however, been responsible for the foundation and maintenance of some of the nation's most famous secondary schools, through the generosity of both its livery companies and far-sighted individuals.

118. Merchant Taylors' School, Suffolk Lane.

119. John Colet, founder of St Paul's School.

St Paul's was founded by John Colet, Dean of St Paul's in 1509. Colet, one of the foremost exponents of the new 'Greek learning' was also a member of the Mercers' Company, which supported his venture. When it was founded its 153 pupils made it the largest school in England. The number was not arbitrary but the traditional number of the catch in the Gospel story of the miraculous draught of fishes and the school took a fish as its symbol. Destroyed in the Great Fire and rebuilt in 1670, it was rebuilt again in 1822, before moving out to Hammersmith in 1884 and on to Barnes in 1968. Old boys of St Paul's include Pepys, Milton, the notorious Judge Jeffreys, the Duke of Marlborough and the astronomer Edmond Halley.

St Paul's Girls' School, another Mercers' foundation, dates from 1904 but was never physically in the City. Its first Director of Music was the composer Gustav Holst.

The Mercers' School was established in 1541 in Old Jewry, possibly on the site of an earlier school dating back to 1447. Burned out in 1666, it occupied various premises until settling in Barnard's Inn in 1894. After a period of severe decline in the eighteenth century, the Mercers' School prospered in Victorian times by offering the sort of education deemed appropriate for the offspring of the commercial and professional classes. It finally closed in 1959.

Christ's Hospital was established by Edward VI on his deathbed as a home for orphans and housed in the former Greyfriars monastery. This was consumed by

120. St Paul's School on the east side of the cathedral.

the Great Fire and replaced by a handsome Wren structure. Distinguished *alumni* include the antiquary William Camden, the Roman Catholic martyr Edmund Campion and the writers Coleridge, Lamb and Leigh Hunt. The girls' department moved out to Hertford in 1704 and the boys to Horsham, Surrey in 1902.

Charterhouse was similarly founded in former monastic buildings, by Thomas Sutton, 'esteemed the richest commoner in England' in 1611. Its roll-call of former pupils includes the essayists Addison and Steele, the eminent jurist Sir William Blackstone, John Wesley, founder of Methodism and Robert Baden-Powell, founder of the Boy Scout movement. The school moved out to Godalming, Surrey in 1874. Part of its premises was taken over by Merchant Taylors' School, which eventually moved out to Middlesex in 1933. Founded in 1561, Merchant Taylors' had stood

in Suffolk Lane, where among its pupils the poet Edmund Spenser and the conspirator Titus Oates had been numbered.

The Sir John Cass Foundation School, confusingly, was actually founded by Zachary Crofton at Houndsditch in 1669 – with money provided by Sir Samuel Stamp. In 1710 Alderman Sir John Cass agreed to top up the school's funds with an endowment but died before signing the requisite document. In 1738 the school closed for a decade before Chancery enforced the deed. In 1869 the school moved to Jewry Street and in 1908 to Duke's Place, where it is now a Church of England primary school. By 1895 the endowment had increased sufficiently to endow a Sir John Cass Technical Institute which successively developed into the City of London Polytechnic and Guildhall University.

The City of London School can trace its ancestry to

121. *Christ's Hospital, otherwise known as the Bluecoat School, built on the site of Greyfriars monastery, Newgate Street. The girls moved out to Hertford in 1778 and the boys to Horsham in 1902.*

the bequest of John Carpenter, Town Clerk of London, who died in 1447. But in its modern form, as a separate school, it dates from 1837. Originally located in Milk Street, it moved to a handsome building on Victoria Embankment in 1883 and to more functional premises at Blackfriars a century later. Its most celebrated former pupils include Liberal Prime Minister H.H. Asquith, children's illustrator Arthur Rackham and novelist Sir Kingsley Amis. The City of London School for Girls opened in 1894 in Carmelite Street and moved in 1973 to the Barbican, the only City-founded secondary school to remain within its boundaries.

Schools founded or funded by City money but outside the City itself include Oundle (Grocers' Company), Bancroft's (Drapers' Company), Haberdashers' Aske's (Haberdashers' Company), Colfe's (Leathersellers' Company), Tonbridge (Skinners' Company) and the City of London Freemen's School. The Stationers' Company school was originally (1858) located in Bolt Court but moved to Hornsey in 1895.

COLLEGES

In 1891 the Goldsmiths' Company sponsored the foundation of Goldsmiths' College at New Cross as a 'Technical and Recreative Institute' in buildings originally designed as a Royal Naval School; it became part of the University of London in 1904. A most important joint initiative by City Livery Companies was the establishment in 1878 of the City and Guilds of London Institute to award certificates of competence for successful completion of courses in technical and commercial subjects. By the mid-twentieth century some 60,000 candidates, including 5,000 from overseas, were taking their 'City and Guilds' in over 150 subjects, ranging from plumbing to hairdressing, at over a thousand different centres. The Guildhall School of Music and Drama (originally of Music only) was founded by the City Corporation in 1880 and opened in Aldermanbury in a disused warehouse where drumming lessons were given in the coal cellar. By 1887 the number of pupils had risen from 62 to 2,500 and the School was occupying purpose-

122. *The south front of Sion College, London Wall, which was rebuilt after the Great Fire.   With its vast library, the College moved to the Victoria Embankment in 1886.*

built premises, designed by Sir Horace Jones, in John Carpenter Street at Blackfriars. The drama section was added in 1935 and the combined institution moved to its present Barbican premises in 1977. City University, which achieved full university status in 1966, was originally founded in 1896 as the North- ampton Polytechnic in Northampton Square to pro- vide courses in engineering, physical sciences and ophthalmic optics.

Sion College is not a college at all but a society of Anglican clergymen with a huge, largely theological library. Founded in 1624 in accordance with the will of Dr. Thomas White, rector of St.Dunstan-in-the- West, the College was intended to promote 'the main- tenance of truth in doctrine, love in conversing to-

gether and ... the repression of such sins as do follow men'. The College and its associated almshouses originally stood in London Wall, a conveniently cen- tral location for its envisaged users, "all the Rectors, Vicars, Lecturers and Clergy in or close to the City". Destroyed in 1666 and rebuilt by 1678, the College moved in 1886 to new mock-Gothic premises de- signed by Arthur Blomfield on Victoria Embank- ment.

Since 1944 the building has been tenanted by the City Livery Club which was founded in 1914 to 'bind together in one organisation liverymen of the various guilds ... in service to the Ancient Corporation and in maintenance of the priceless City churches.'

123. *The inner courtyard of the Belle Sauvage, Ludgate Hill.*

Eating and Drinking

BELLE SAUVAGE AND BOAR'S HEAD

An English pub is no mere beer-shop, a London pub still less so. Over the course of centuries a single pub may play many parts. On Ludgate Hill once stood Savage's Inn, first mentioned in 1452. Before there were theatres as such, plays were performed in its courtyard. The Indian princess, Pocahontas, was a guest there in 1616-17. In honour of her visit its name was changed to the Belle Sauvage. Entertainment continued to feature as one of its attractions, for in 1683 the curious could go there to view a 'Rynoceros lately brought from the West Indies'. In the eighteenth century it was one of the largest of the coaching-inns, along with the Swan with Two Necks (originally Two Nicks) in Lad Lane (now Gresham Street) and the Bull and Mouth (originally Boulogne Mouth) in St Martin's le Grand. The Belle Sauvage was demol-

ished in 1873 to make way for the printing works of Cassell, Petter and Galpin, which was blitzed in 1940.

Another public house of comparable distinction was the Boar's Head, which once stood in Great Eastcheap and was mentioned as early as the reign of Richard II. Boswell affirmed it to be Falstaff's tavern. Goldsmith wrote there. In 1784 Pitt and Wilberforce attended the last annual dinner held there to honour Shakespeare. Later it became a gunsmith's before being demolished in 1831 to make way for the new approaches to Rennie's rebuilt London Bridge.

THE INNER MAN

The reputations of particular hostelries were often founded on the specific excellence of their food and drink. The Woolsack in Aldgate was famed for pies in Ben Jonson's day but would later be eclipsed in that respect by Ye Olde Cheshire Cheese whose unique puddings, incorporating beefsteaks, kidneys, oysters, larks and mushrooms, ran to eighty pounds in

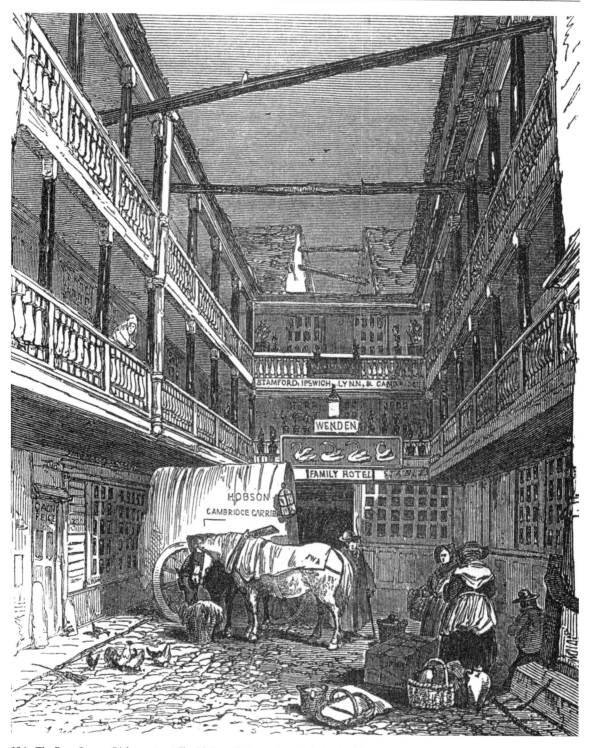

124. *The Four Swans, Bishopsgate, still with its galleries, and proclaiming itself a 'family hotel', in 1848.*

weight and were mentioned in Galsworthy's *Forsyte Saga*. The London Tavern in Bishopsgate had a dining room which could accommodate 355 and regularly hosted the official dinners of the East India Company. The Magpie, located in the same street, added 'and Punchbowl' to its name after it became the watering-hole of Whig politicians, who drank punch in contrast with the Tories' claret. At the Salutation in Newgate Street, Coleridge and Lamb met to chat over 'Welsh rarebit, egg-hot and orinoco'. The Shades off Upper Thames Street was allegedly the last house to serve wine the old-fashioned way, straight from the butt in silver tankards.

WHAT'S IN A NAME?

Many pubs owe their interest, and sometimes their name, to a specific event or association. The Hand and Shears in Cloth Fair was, in the sixteenth century, home to a 'Piepowder Court' where stall-holders

125. *The Bolt in Tun, Fleet Street.*

126. *Dirty Dick's, Bishopsgate, in the 1920s.*

could receive instant justice in cases of dispute. Its sign commemorates the ceremony of cutting a piece of cloth, by which the Lord Mayor traditionally opened Smithfield's annual fair. The Three Tuns in Guildhall Yard served in 1660 as the military headquarters of General Monck, whose support was decisive in the restoration of Charles II. The King's Head in Fleet Street was reputedly the clandestine meeting-place of Titus Oates and his fellow-conspirators, later executed for allegedly plotting the assassination of the same monarch. Williamson's Tavern, off Bow Lane, once served as the official residence of the Lord Mayor. It became a pub in 1739 and has a plaque in its parlour to mark the exact centre of the City. Dirty Dick's in Bishopsgate is said to have derived its theme of dusty decay from the dandyish Nathaniel Bentley, who renounced both housekeeping and personal hygiene after the death of his fiancée on their wedding eve. The Magpie and Stump on the south side of Old Bailey was once famed as the best vantage-point for viewing public hangings. It was also a tavern in which one of the clubs that championed the Hanoverian succession met.

Architecturally City pubs can boast more often of interest than of excellence, though Ye Olde Watling in Watling Street is, perhaps predictably, credited to Wren himself as an accommodation for craftsmen working on St Paul's. The Hoop and Grapes at Aldgate may date from the thirteenth century and has medi-

127. *The Hoop and Grapes in Aldgate, its name deriving from the local wine trade.*

128. *The Bell, Addle Hill in 1868; watercolour by J.T. Wilson.*

eval cellars to back its claim, although Pevsner dates
the actual building to the late seventeenth century.
The *Lord Raglan*, originally the Bush, in St Martin's le
Grand, has cellars incorporating part of the encircling
wall of Roman Londinium. The Windmill in Old
Jewry was built on a former synagogue. The Old Bell
Inn in Fleet Street, rebuilt by Wren in 1678, was said
to be on the site of the printing shop of Wynkyn de
Worde, Caxton's apprentice and successor. The cellars of the Viaduct Tavern, itself named in honour of
the opening of the Holborn Viaduct in 1869, were
once part of Newgate prison. The Art Nouveau
Blackfriar takes its name from the Dominican monastery on whose site it stands.

*129. Ye Olde Cheshire Cheese, Wine Office Court, Fleet
Street; drawing by Arthur Moreland, 1931. Over the
fireplace on the ground floor is a portrait of a waiter, resting a
hand on the table to the right of the fireplace which, legend has
it, was that usually chosen by Dickens.*

LITERARY PUBS

Three City pubs were famed as the home of noted
literary circles. At the Devil in Fleet Street Ben Jonson
founded the Apollo Club. The Devil was later patron-
ised by Samuel Johnson and demolished in 1788 to
make way for an extension of Child's Bank. At the
Mermaid in Bread Street Sir Walter Ralegh founded a
club whose members included Shakespeare, Jonson,
Donne, Beaumont and Fletcher. The Mermaid was
engulfed by the Great Fire in 1666 but its fame lin-
gered to inspire a tribute from Keats:

Souls of poets dead and gone
What Elysium have ye known.
Happy field or mossy cavern
Choicer than the Mermaid Tavern?

Ye Olde Cheshire Cheese in Wine Office Court, off
Fleet Street, was the favoured haunt of Johnson's
circle – Reynolds, Gibbon, Garrick, Boswell and Gold-

130. The Dick Whittington Tavern in Cloth Fair, West Smithfield; painting by James S. Ogilvy, 1910.

131. The rebuilt King Lud on the corner of Ludgate Circus; from The Builder, *1 April 1871.*

smith. In Dickens' time it was well known not only to him but also to his friends Leech, Forster, Cruikshank and Wilkie Collins as well as Carlyle, Macaulay, Tennyson, Thackeray and Hood. A generation later it was visited by Beerbohm, Chesterton and Conan Doyle and such literary pilgrims as Mark Twain and Theodore Roosevelt. It also hosted the meetings of a group of poets known as the 'Rhymers' whose outstanding talent was W.B. Yeats.

City pubs figure as settings in the novels of Charles Dickens. The George and Vulture in St Michael's Court provided lodging for Mr Pickwick and when the same hero was incarcerated in the Fleet prison he sent to the Horn Tavern in Knightrider Street for two bottles of good wine. In 1841 Dickens presided over a meeting for the benefit of the Sanatorium for Sick Authors and Artists at the London Tavern in Bishopsgate and in 1851 over the annual dinner held there in aid of the General Theatrical Fund. The same London Tavern features in *Nicholas Nickleby* as the venue for a meeting on behalf of the 'United Metropolitan Improved Hot Muffin and Crumpet Baking and Punctual Delivery Company'. The hero of that novel meets his dreadful one-eyed employer, Wackford

Squeers, in the coffee-room of the Saracen's Head, a famed and ancient coaching inn on Snow Hill.

COFFEE HOUSES

A blue plaque in St Michael's Alley, off Cornhill, proclaims that 'Here stood the first London Coffee House at the Sign of Pasqua Rosee's Head 1652'. Pasqua Rosee, a native of Dubrovnik, was the servant of a merchant named Edwards who acquired a taste for coffee while trading in Smyrna (now Izmir, Turkey). On returning to London he continued to indulge and shortly afterwards set his man up in business on his own account. The sales pitch for the new drink was strongly health-oriented – "it is a very good help to digestion, quickens the spirits and is good against sore eyes."

Over the next two centuries hundreds more coffee-houses flourished, especially around Cornhill and Fleet Street. Providing venues for the leisurely spread of gossip and information, coffee-houses served as snack bars, job centres, travel agencies, post offices and gentlemen's clubs and were intimately associated with the emergence of such institutions as ma-

132. *Garraway's Coffee House, Exchange Alley, Cornhill. It began in 1669 and was frequented by fur traders of the Hudson's Bay Company. Thomas Garraway was reputed to be the first man in England to sell tea, advocating its qualities 'for the cure of all disorders'.*

rine and fire insurance, Lloyd's and the Stock Exchange. They did not, however, win immediate acceptance. Ex-barber James Farr, having converted Fleet Street's Rainbow Tavern into a coffee-house of the same name, found himself in 1657 accused of causing 'Disorder and Annoys' because the preparation of coffee repelled his neighbours with 'evil smells' and constituted a grave fire risk into the bargain. Perhaps the neighbours had a point. Hain's, in Birchin Lane, perished in the conflagration which swept Cornhill in 1748; Jonathan's of Exchange Alley was also destroyed at the same time but was rebuilt, only to meet its final fiery doom thirty years later. John's, 'greatly scorched' in 1748, went up in flames with the Royal Exchange in 1838. New Jonathan's, established above the Stock Exchange in Threadneedle Street in 1773, continued to attract jobbers after its relocation to Capel Court until it too burned down in 1816.

Specific coffee-houses frequently became associated with a particular type of clientéle. Hogarth's father bankrupted himself by sinking his capital into a spectacularly futile attempt at niche marketing – a coffee-house in which all the customers would be required to speak Latin. Batson's, established at 17 Cornhill in the 1690s, was, according to the *London Gazette* "much frequented by men of intelligence for conversation" but became especially noted for physicians, who were observed to "flock together like birds of prey watching for carcases." Child's in Warwick Lane, being near the College of Physicians, also attracted medical practitioners, as well as lawyers and clergymen. Boswell often went there, as well as to the nearby St Paul's, where a club of clerics and doctors met for conversation on Thursdays. Booksellers resorted to the aptly-named Chapter coffee-house in Paternoster Row. Nando's, in Fleet Street, was mostly the haunt of lawyers, including one Edward Thurlow, whose student liaison with its barmaid lasted until her death and produced two bastard children but did not prevent him from becoming Lord Chancellor of England.

The Jerusalem in Cowper's Court was, according to William Hickey in 1776, "the general resort of all those who had anything to do with India" and especially employees of the East India Company. The Jamaica in St Michael's Alley was the natural focus for Caribbean traders and acted as a postal-drop and pick-up point for their correspondence as well as an enquiry point for intending passengers to the West Indies. Unsurprisingly renowned for the excellence of its rum, it became the Jamaica Wine House in 1869. The Virginia and Maryland in nearby Newman's Court was similarly converted into a tavern in 1838.

One of the most enduring of all coffee-houses was Dick's, near Temple Bar, which, paradoxically, may have owed its survival to its relative independence from City custom. Opened in 1680, it came to rely on

a steady trade from country gentlemen and survived until 1885, when it became a French restaurant.

Garraway's, established in 1669 in Exchange Alley, became famed as an auction house, initially for Hudson's Bay Company furs and later for sugar, coffee, textiles, spices, ships and salvaged goods. The enterprising proprietor was England's first retailer of tea, which he liberally recommended as "the cure of all disorders", although he also offered his customers pale ale, punch, sherry and cherry wine. By the early nineteenth century Garraway's was hosting the business of estate agents, drug brokers and 'Turkey merchants'. Defoe and Swift both referred to Garraway's and Dickens mentioned it in *Pickwick Papers, Martin Chuzzlewit, Little Dorrit* and *The Uncommercial Traveller*. Closed down in 1872, it was subsequently demolished to make way for Martin's Bank.

The London Coffee-House, next to St Martin's church on Ludgate Hill, was not opened until 1731 and was initially known as Ashley's London Punch House. Boswell noted that its intellectual clientéle was "composed principally of physicians, dissenting clergy and masters of academies." Masonic meetings were also held there and a strong American connection developed over the years. Benjamin Franklin attended a discussion club there and so did the scientist Joseph Priestley, who later fled to exile in America. Following the Great Exhibition of 1851 the financier and philanthropist George Peabody chose the London as the venue for a dinner to celebrate American success in the Great Exhibition. Closed as a coffee-house in 1867, the London is now the Olde London Tavern.

133. *Grigsby's Coffee House.*

Lawyers and their Quarters

THE TEMPLE

Legal London developed along the strategically-placed corridor linking the commercial City and royal Westminster. Its core is the Temple, which takes its name from the Knights Templar, an order of crusaders, who lived as monks and fought as warriors. Founded in 1118, their initial purpose was to provide armed escorts for pilgrims to the Holy Land, but they subsequently came to offer a wide range of more secular security services such as guarding and transferring bullion. Established in England during the reign of Henry I (1100-35), the Templars in 1185 built a substantial headquarters and distinctive round church by the banks of the Thames, off Fleet Street. Modelled on the church of the Holy Sepulchre (or possibly the Dome of the Rock) in Jerusalem, it was consecrated by Heraclius, the Patriarch of that city, in the presence of Henry II. The pointed arches of the Temple church, combined with the semi-circular of its Romanesque work point forward to the emerging Gothic style known as Early English. A rectangular choir was added in 1204. There was also a side-chapel, but the crypt, in which secret initiation ceremonies were conducted, is all that survives of this. The Templars accumulated great wealth and excited great envy. Discredited in a series of show-trials for every vice from blasphemy to sodomy, they were dissolved in 1312 and their property passed over to another military order, the Knights of the Hospital of St John of Jerusalem. As the Hospitallers already had a large estate on the northern edge of the City, at Clerkenwell, they were happy to lease the Temple to lawyers, who found it an extremely convenient location, midway between their clients residing in the City and the king's courts located in Westminster Hall. The original buildings may have been convenient but do not seem to have been particularly defensible. Lawyers were high on the list of hate-figures for the mob during the Peasants' Revolt of 1381, so many were slaughtered out of hand and all their documentation, which constituted the outward forms of servile bondage, were incinerated

Lawyers continued as tenants of the Temple, but after 1540 of the Crown. A practical distinction was made between the Inner and Middle Temple but no formal division took place until 1732. An area known as Outer Temple once formed part of the Templars' property but was never occupied by lawyers.

In 1573 Middle Temple completed the construction of a handsome brick hall, with a mighty double

134. Temple church.

hammer-beam roof and an elaborately-carved oak screen. This building was used for dining, lectures, the pseudo-trials known as moots, revels, masques and, on 2 February 1601, the premiere of *Twelfth Night* in the presence of Elizabeth I, probably with Shakespeare himself among the cast. Until 1830 a large open fire stood at the centre of the Hall. The 29-foot 'Bench table' and accompanying 'Cupboard' (an associated, smaller table, used in debates) survive from the sixteenth century, as do the roof and screen, despite severe damage in the Blitz.

In 1608, James I turned over the freehold of the Temple to its occupants, a decision that he and his successors might subsequently have regretted, considering how prominent a part lawyers, notably the implacable Sir Edward Coke (1552-1634), an Inner Temple man, took in the constitutional struggles which plagued the monarchy for the rest of that century. Ireton, Cromwell's general, was a Middle Temple man - but so was the Earl of Clarendon, the Crown's staunchest supporter and historian of 'the Great Rebellion'.

Having survived the Great Fire of 1666, which petered out further down Fleet Street, Middle Temple was seriously damaged by its own conflagration in 1678, when the freezing of the Thames made it virtu-

135. *Inner Temple Gatehouse on Fleet Street. The building is now more commonly known as 'Prince Henry's Room', from the Prince of Wales feathers on the ceiling of the main room above the gateway. The gatehouse (part of which was occupied by a public house), was reconstructed c.1610 - the year in which Prince Henry, son of James I, became Prince of Wales.*

136. *G. E. Street, a perfectionist, whose pupils included William Morris, Philip Webb and Norman Shaw..*

ally impossible to combat the flames. The reconstructions included a new gateway onto Fleet Street, often attributed to Wren but actually the work of Roger North, a Bencher (senior, ruling member) of Middle Temple, whom Professor Pevsner mischievously refers to as *another* amateur.

Perhaps the most influential of all the Temple lawyers was Sir William Blackstone (1723-80), whose magisterial four-volume *Commentaries on the Laws of England* (1765-9) became a basic source-book for the 'Founding Fathers' who drafted the constitution of the United States. In the composition of the final volume Blackstone was persistently distracted by the raucous parties of his upstairs neighbour, the writer Oliver Goldsmith (1728-74). As Goldsmith died and was buried in Middle Temple, contemplating his tombstone may have afforded the eminent jurist some wintry satisfaction.

The tranquil gardens of the Temple appear to have been just that throughout their long existence, never built upon or cultivated commercially. Tradition holds that it was in Middle Temple Gardens that a red rose and a white were first plucked by the contending dynastic houses of Lancaster and York, whose thirty year conflict thus became known as the Wars of the Roses. The Great Spring Show of the Royal Horticultural Society was held in Inner Temple Gardens from 1888 to until, 1913 when it moved up-river to become the Chelsea Flower Show.

137. *Pump Court, Middle Temple; Drawing by Arthur Moreland, 1931.*

CITY COURTS

Opposite the Temple stand the Royal Courts of Justice, completed in 1882 after driving their architect, G.E. Street (1824-81) to a premature grave. The sheer scale of the project – a thousand rooms and 35,000,000 bricks – compounded by bad weather, labour disputes and budgetary problems brought on a fatal stroke. It is often remarked that this is the only secular building in London to bear a statue of Christ, here depicted as the Lawgiver, between Solomon and Alfred. Perhaps he was also Street's Redeemer.

Round the corner in Chancery Lane stands the headquarters of the Law Society, the solicitors' professional body, which was preceded by the 'Society of Gentlemen Practisers in the Several Courts of Law and Equity', founded in 1739. The neo-classical building was designed by Lewis Vulliamy in 1831. Opposite, in complete contrast, stands the great Gothic pile of the Public Record Office, built to the designs of Sir James Pennethorne between 1851-66.

The present Central Criminal Court dates only from 1907 but there was an Old Bailey Sessions House beside Newgate prison as early as 1539. Celebrated trials held in the modern building include those of Dr Crippen (1910), Peter Sutcliffe, the 'Yorkshire Ripper' (1981) and the Nazi propagandist William Joyce ('Lord Haw-Haw') (1945). Technically the judges of this court include all Aldermen of the City as well as its Recorder and Common Serjeant, both posts once held by the infamous Judge Jeffreys (1644-89).

Criminal City

CRIMINALS AND POLICE

Medieval Londoners dealt with pickpockets and shop-lifters with the rough justice of the hue and cry, while constables and watchmen in each Ward kept uncouth neighbours, drunks and rowdy apprentices under restraint. Cheating craftsmen and shopkeepers, a perennial problem for a commercial city, were dealt with by fines and the humiliation of the hurdle or the stocks. By the seventeenth century the City's militia, the trained bands, could be called out to maintain order when customary festivals threatened to turn riotous. Organized crime emerged at around the same time, with the streets south of Fleet Street its main spawning-ground. Transvestite 'Moll Cutpurse', pickpocket, forger, fence and mugger, lived and died there "within two doors of the Globe Tavern over against the Conduit."

The notorious 'thief-taker' Jonathan Wild (?1682-1725) ran half of London's underworld, pretending to recover stolen goods while in fact usually being the one who had had them stolen in the first place. From 1719 until his luck ran out, Wild lived in a fine house in Old Bailey, in the very shadow of Newgate prison, a prototype of the modern gangster, operating a viciously exploitative network of operations behind the seemingly respectable facade of a businessman and public benefactor. The parallel runs even further, because Wild was finally condemned on a legal tech-nicality and hanged for accepting a reward for goods he knew to be stolen.

The precariousness of public order was grossly exposed during the anti-Catholic Gordon riots of 1780, when the mob forced open the prisons and looted the distilleries in an orgy of destruction which threatened the Bank of England itself and was only put down by the use of troops, with the loss of hundreds of lives. In 1784 a City Day Police was formed as a result of the riots and later supplemented by a Night Police. But the City Corporation, jealous of its independence, for half a century repeatedly blocked initiatives to establish a proper police force for the capital as a whole, until the Metropolitan Police Act of 1829 conceded that the City should continue to make its own separate arrangements. A separate City of London police force finally came into being a decade later, in 1839, with its headquarters in a former mer-chant's house at 26 Old Jewry. When Parliament attempted to abolish this in 1863 the successful cam-paign of resistance was led by the Governor of the Bank of England himself. Probably the most famous incident in the history of the City force was the Houndsditch murders of 1910, when anarchists rob-bing a jeweller's shop shot and killed three officers –

138. An Elizabethan bellman. From Dekker's Belman of London *(1608)*

and were subsequently traced to Sidney Street in the East End, where at least two of them perished in a fire following a siege and gun-battle.

PRISONS

The Fleet Prison is first recorded in the late twelfth century but may have been a century older. It was particularly used to incarcerate those who had in-curred royal displeasure and debtors. The poet John Donne was detained there to punish his elopement and dramatist William Wycherley was imprisoned for debt, as was William Penn. Throughout the eight-eenth century prisoners in the Fleet remained notori-ously vulnerable to extortion and maltreatment at the hands of the prison keepers, as well as of their fellow inmates. Dickens' graphic description of the Fleet in *Pickwick Papers* was written on the eve of its closure (1842) and demolition (1846).

There was certainly a prison at Newgate by the twelfth century and money was left in Dick Whittington's will for its renovation. Rebuilt again two centuries later and again after the Great Fire, its imposing frontage of 1672 included a statue of Whittington and his cat. Inside it was a hell-hole of filth, foulness, brutality and infection. Its inmates included highwayman Claude Duval, conspirator Titus Oates, Quaker William Penn and journalist Daniel Defoe. Jonathan Wild was held there for trial and execution in 1725. So was the Houdini-like Jack Sheppard, who beat handcuffs, manacles, chains, locked doors and a sixty foot drop to escape (briefly)

139. Fleet Prison, by Pugin and Rowlandson, c.1808.

and become a London celebrity. Rebuilt by George Dance the Younger in 1770-8, Newgate was utterly destroyed in the Gordon riots of 1780 and had to be rebuilt by Dance again. It remained so degraded in its conditions, however, that it provided the inspiration for the prison reforms of the crusading Quaker, Elizabeth Fry (1780-1845). Newgate was finally demolished in 1902 to make way for the Central Criminal Court (Old Bailey).

The Tun on Cornhill, shaped like an over-sized wine-cask, was built by Lord Mayor Henry le Walleis in 1282 for the detention of 'night walkers' and later used to hold cheating bakers and millers and priests caught in flagrante with women.

Another medieval foundation was the Bread Street Compter (pronounced counter), controlled by the City Sheriff and used for the confinement of debtors. In 1555 its inmates were moved to a new compter in Wood Street and in 1791 from there to its successor in Giltspur Street, until it too was demolished in 1855. The oldest City compter, at Poultry, mainly held

prisoners committed by the Lord Mayor; it was demolished in 1817. By then debtors could be transferred to the newly-built prison at Whitecross Street, which had been specifically constructed to separate debtors from regular criminals. It was demolished in 1870 and its site is now covered by the Barbican.

Part of Ludgate became a prison in the reign of Richard II. Debtors regularly bawled through the windows at passers-by for charity. The gate and prison were demolished in 1760.

Bridewell began its life as a palace built for Henry VIII between 1515 and 1520 at the junction of the Fleet river and the Thames. Emperor Charles V was lavishly entertained there in 1522. A decade later Holbein painted *The Ambassadors* there, when it was leased to the French ambassador. In 1553 Edward VI turned Bridewell over to the City to be used as an orphanage, a hostel for vagrants and a 'house of correction' for petty offenders and loose women. Bridewell specialised in the 'short, sharp shock' approach to criminality and routinely included public flogging in its regime,

140. *Newgate Prison, by Thomas H. Shepherd.*

141. *Inside the chapel at Newgate Prison, by Pugin and Rowlandson. It was the custom of the gaolers to raise extra money for themselves by charging members of the public to view condemned prisoners at their last chapel service before execution.*

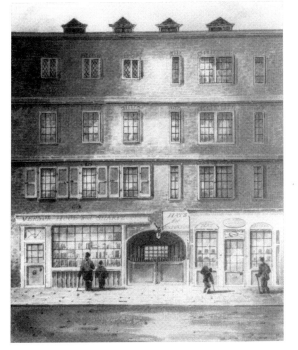

142. (Above) Giltspur Compter in Giltspur Street. Built at the end of the 18th century, it was demolished in 1855.

143. (Left) Poultry Compter, approached between a row of shops. It was the oldest of the compters and used for the prisoners of the Lord Mayor. It was demolished in 1817.

as well as having a riverside ducking-stool and stocks. Blue-uniformed Bridewell orphans were apprenticed to a trade and later often packed off to the American colonies. Rebuilt after 1666, Bridewell was in advance of other institutions in appointing a prison doctor in 1700 (75 years before any other prison) and from 1788 onwards providing straw for bedding. It closed in 1855 and was demolished in 1863-4.

SANCTUARIES AND ROOKERIES
Traditional criminal sanctuaries at the former religious houses of St Martin-le-Grand and Whitefriars survived the Reformation because the law was too weak in practice to suppress them. Rookeries of slums, impenetrable to law officers, served as breeding-grounds for crime around the fringes of the City at the Mint, Houndsditch, Barbican, Smithfield and Saffron Hill until well into the nineteenth century.

Father Figures

The modern City is so dominated by vast, impersonal institutions that it is easy to forget that many of them owe their origins to specific personalities, founders of business dynasties or corporations which for generations often perpetuated their names and sometimes the imprint of their character as well.

The names of London's earliest banks remind us of their founders. Hoare's was founded by goldsmith Richard Hoare around 1672. Francis Child, another goldsmith, founded a rival house soon after. Coutts & Co., however, was originally founded in 1692 by John Campbell at 'the sign of The Three Crowns in the Strand' and it is this original sign and the name of Campbell, rather than Coutts and the later royal connection, that is perpetuated in the bank's current logo.

FOUNDER OF THE NATIONAL GALLERY
Born in St Petersburg, John Julius Angerstein (1735-1823) was at work in a City counting-house at the age of fifteen, became an underwriter at Lloyd's when barely twenty-one and before he was forty had built a handsome villa to live in at Blackheath. 'Woodlands' was renowned for its lavish hospitality and its comfort, becoming the first private residence in Britain since Roman times to have central heating. Visitors could also feast their eyes on its owner's superb collection of Old Master paintings, selected with the advice of the Regency's leading portraitist, Sir Thomas Lawrence. After Angerstein's death his collection became the nucleus of the National Gallery and went on display to the public in his London residence in Pall Mall until William Wilkins' gallery building was completed.

SIXTH POWER IN EUROPE
It was the Duc de Richelieu who declared that "There are six great powers in Europe: England, France, Prussia, Austria, Russia and Baring Brothers....". The founder of the dynasty, Sir Francis Baring (1740-1810), was the grandson of a German immigrant cloth manufacturer and not only founded the banking house but also became a director of the East India Company. His son Alexander (1774-1848) extended the bank's operations to the United States – and fortunately took on a workaholic American, Joshua Bates (1788-1864), to revitalize this core business while he turned to politics. As Baron Ashburton, Alexander was chiefly responsible for negotiating a resolution to the dispute between the US and Britain over the border between Canada and Maine. Bates eventually became a British citizen and was knighted for his philanthropy. Described by one contemporary as "ignorant and illiterate", he was, ironically, the founder of the Boston Public Library. What he took real pride in, however, was the feeling that "it *is* something to be at the head of the first commercial House in the World." Francis's grandsons achieved

144. Julius Angerstein.

145. Sir Richard Hoare.

distinction in varying spheres – one as Bishop of Durham, another as Chancellor of the Exchequer and a third, Evelyn Baring, Earl of Cromer, as benevolent despot of British-occupied Egypt. The iconoclastic biographer Lytton Strachey grudgingly conceded of Cromer that "his ambition can be stated in a single phrase: it was, to become an institution; and he achieved it." Much the same could have been said of the family as a whole.

PROVERBIAL WEALTH

The fortunes attributed to the Rothschilds were so large that their name passed into proverbial usage as a synonym for millionaire. The founder of the dynasty, Meyer Amschel Rothschild (1743-1812) was a Frankfurt money-lender whose eldest son took over the business while the other four dispersed to Vienna, Paris, Naples and London. In London Nathan Meyer (1777-1836) made himself indispensable to the British government in organising the financing of Wellington's Peninsular campaigns and after the war capitalised on his political and overseas connections to extend his fortune by raising foreign loans. He freely admitted his obsession with work – "I do not read books, I do not play cards, I do not go to the theatre, my only pleasure is my business." He was equally candid in his opinion of his adopted countrymen, reassuring his brothers that "as long as we have a

good business and are rich, everybody will flatter us." And he warned his children that "it requires a great deal of boldness, and a great deal of caution, to make a great fortune; and when you have got it, it requires ten times as much wit to keep it."

Nathan's successor, Liônel (1808-79), was to play a crucial role in the enlargement of civil liberties. Elected to Parliament in 1847, 1849, 1852 and 1857, he was on each occasion barred from taking his seat because, as a Jew, his religion precluded him from taking the required oath of loyalty 'in the true faith of a Christian'. Instrumental in securing the removal of this obstacle in 1858, he sat as an MP from then until 1868 and from 1869 to 1874. Lionel's brother, Sir Anthony de Rothschild (1810-76), served in 1870 as first President of London's new United Synagogue and his son, Sir Nathan Meyer (1840-1915), became in 1885 the first Jewish member of the House of Lords. 'Natty' did much to ease the adjustment to life in Britain of Jewish immigrants from Poland and Russia by sponsoring hostels, housing, schools and soup kitchens. In business his watchword was caution – "I go to the bank every morning and when I say 'no' I return home at night without a worry. But when I say 'yes' it's like putting your finger into a machine – the whirring wheels may drag your whole body in after the finger." As war brutally disrupted the smooth operations of finance in the year of his death, Lord Rothschild gamely declared that "I've got to keep breathing; it'll be my worst business mistake if I don't."

FATHER OF PHILANTHROPY

When Andrew Carnegie was asked who had inspired his legendary generosity to good causes, he replied "George Peabody". Unlike Carnegie, a Scottish immigrant, George Peabody (1795-1869) was a fourth-generation American, born and raised in Danvers, Massachusetts. Fatherless at sixteen, with only four years of elementary education behind him, Peabody took on financial responsibility for his widowed mother and family and paid off all their debts. His life from then on was a classic story of success through diligence and enterprise. Having built a sound fortune in the 'dry goods' trade, he established a British branch of Peabody, Riggs & Co. at 31 Moorgate Street in 1837. Five years later Peabody was ready to shift the balance of his business from commerce into finance, specialising in American securities. Long hours, attention to detail, a prodigious memory and a steady nerve enabled Peabody not merely to survive but to prosper through the periodic panics which beset the mid-Victorian City. Although a millionaire, bachelor Peabody continued to live in rented accommodation and to take sandwiches to the office for lunch; his only personal indulgences were angling and a taste for Scottish country music.

But when it came to promoting America's standing

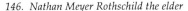

146. Nathan Meyer Rothschild the elder

147. George Peabody.

in British eyes, Peabody was far-sighted and generous. After Congress failed to vote funds to back
American exhibitors at the Great Exhibition of 1851,
he put up the money out of his own pocket. In the
same year he inaugurated an annual Independence
Day dinner, a social triumph, attended by more than
a thousand guests, with the venerated Duke of Wellington himself as guest of honour.

In 1854 Peabody's firm moved to 22 Old Broad
Street and Junius S. Morgan was taken on as a partner.
The firms of Morgan Grenfell, J.P. Morgan and
Morgan Stanley are all lineal descendants of this
partnership.

The year 1862 marked Queen Victoria's silver jubilee and Peabody's twenty-fifth year in the City. He
decided to mark the occasion with an unprecedented
gesture, donating £150,000 for the benefit of London's
poor. More important still, he established a board of
trustees to devise and administer the programme,
thus in effect inventing the modern charitable foundation. Further grants eventually topped up Peabody's
gift to the half million mark. The money was spent on
housing for the industrious and respectable poor,
those who were employed but might easily slip into
the underclass without the security of a decent and
well-managed environment. The first Peabody Estate

of three blocks of apartments was built in Spitalfields,
on the very edge of the City, less than a mile from
Peabody's own offices.

Peabody's open-handed gesture seized the imagination of the Victorian Establishment. Queen Victoria let it be known that a baronetcy or the Order of the
Bath were his for the asking. But patriotic Peabody
declined to change his nationality in order to accept a
foreign honour and graciously contented himself with
a framed portrait of the monarch and a personal letter
of thanks, acknowledging his "noble act of more than
princely munificence," an act "wholly without parallel". The City itself responded with an act wholly
without parallel, and made Peabody the first American to receive its Freedom. Since his day there has
only been a second – Dwight D. Eisenhower. In 1869
Peabody was further honoured by a statue, unveiled
by the Prince of Wales himself. Peabody's funeral that
same year brought London to a standstill as he was
afforded yet another unique accolade – temporary
interment in the nave of Westminster Abbey. A month
later his casket was carried back to the United States
aboard *HMS Monarch*, the pride of the Royal Navy, to
be laid to rest in his place of birth – now renamed
Peabody in his honour. Peabody's donations on both
sides of the Atlantic amounted to $8,566,960, a sum
reckoned to be equivalent in modern terms to more
than £63,000,000. In the year of the bi-centenary of his
birth over 27,000 Londoners were still living in housing managed by the Peabody Trust.

148. George Williams.

SPIRITUAL CAPITALIST
Somerset-born George Williams (1821-1905) discovered God at sixteen and at twenty found himself working, as one of a hundred and fifty assistants, in a draper's and haberdasher's at 72 St Paul's Churchyard. Working from seven in the morning till nine at night, his colleagues took their only recreation in the Goose and Gridiron, where they could pass their few off-duty hours in drinking, gambling, smoking and swearing. Determined to combat this futile dissolution, on 6 June 1844 George Williams convened a meeting of thirteen fellow-Christians in his dormitory for the 'purpose of establishing a society which should have for its object the arousing of converted men in the different drapery Establishments in the Metropolis to a sense of their obligation and responsibility as Christians in diffusing religious knowledge to those around them.' And thus the Young Men's Christian Association was born. Williams was knighted in the year of its golden jubilee.

INTEGRITY, IMPARTIALITY
Born in Kassel, Israel Beer Josaphat (1816-99) became a Christian in 1844, adopting the name Paul Julius Reuter. As a clerk in his uncle's Gottingen bank, Reuter became acquainted with the physicist Carl Friedrich Gauss, after pointing out a serious error in a money transaction he had made. Gauss was a lecturer at the local university, experimenting with the electric telegraph and his interest alerted the young clerk to the revolutionary potential of the new communications technology. Moving on to Berlin, where he married a banker's daughter and thus acquired access to capital which enabled him to go into publishing, Reuter found it prudent to move on yet again to Paris in 1848. Here he began to work as a foreign correspondent for various German newspapers and took his first steps towards establishing a business of news-diffusion by using carrier-pigeons and the electric telegraph. In 1850 he set up a carrier-pigeon service between Aachen and Brussels, the terminal points of the German and French-Belgian telegraph lines. The pigeons beat the leisurely mail-train by hours but the gap between the lines was soon closed and Reuter had to move on again.

In 1851 Julius Reuter established a telegraphic office in London, at No. 1 Royal Exchange Buildings, one of the first purpose-built office-blocks in the City. Initially his main business was transmitting commercial data for banks and brokerage houses, but in 1858 he acquired his first newspaper as a subscriber, the *Morning Advertiser*. In 1859 he pulled off a major news coup, transmitting to London the text of a speech by

149. Paul Julius Reuter.

Napoleon III presaging war with Austria over Italy. Many more newspapers, who could not afford to keep their own correspondents overseas, joined the list of Reuter's subscribers. In 1858 they paid £30 a month; ten years later they were glad to pay £1,000 a year. With the completion of the Atlantic cable in 1866, Reuter was able to benefit from the expansion of business between Britain and the United States during the great boom which followed the ending of the civil war. Created a Baron by the Duke of Saxe-Coburg-Gotha in 1871, twenty years later he was accorded the same rank in Britain, where he had taken out citizenship. Ironically, in view of the founder's determination to be 'a truth teller, unbiased by political or special interests', Reuter's employees were later to include two masters of fantastical fiction – Edgar Wallace, creator of King Kong, and Ian Fleming, creator of James Bond.

The Capitalists

THE SOUTH SEA BUBBLE .... AND AFTER

The eighteenth-century City of London was already a predominantly commercial city but its capitalist operations, although increasingly global in orientation, were still constrained by ancient guild regulations, state monopolies and entrenched interests.

The 'South Sea Bubble' episode, which culminated in 1720, aptly illustrates the then weakness of impersonal institutions compared with personal relationships. The South Seas Trading Company was the creation of factional court politics, not a City initiative. Its commercial prospects rested on a diplomatic agreement between Britain and Spain which gave it a monopoly of the trade in slaves and European goods with Spanish-ruled South America. In the long run, these prospects might have been sound enough, had the diplomatic serenity which guaranteed their framework endured – a dubious proposition. Unfortunately a corrupt administration and a naive investing public unwittingly conspired to create a classic speculative bubble. To get the scheme going politicians gave friends and contacts the chance to get in early by offering them shares, often at a discount, sometimes free. As share-prices rose dizzyingly, investors sold solid assets, including whole landed estates, so that they, too, could cash in. When the crash came hundreds of fortunes and reputations were ruined and Parliament hastily passed legislation severely restricting the promotion and operation of joint-stock ventures. The one good thing that did come out of the whole wretched business was Guy's Hospital, founded by benevolent Cornhill bookseller Thomas Guy, who had the prudence to bail out just before the crash and make a killing.

Partnerships therefore remained the norm in business for the next century. Trust and honour in the most literal and personal sense were the basis of survival and prosperity in the intimate world where deals were struck along the various 'walks' of the Royal Exchange or across the tables of coffee-houses, and sealed with a handshake and a bumper of sherry. It mattered very much whom you knew and whom you married. In a volatile commercial world, where credit in every sense was crucial, a sound network of well-heeled in-laws and cousins could prove vital in a crisis. Many such bonds were further strengthened by ties of race or religion, especially among Jews, Quakers and others whose faith barred them from service to the Anglican state or in the professions and thus virtually impelled them towards trade and finance. Partly as a consequence of the restrictions on joint-stock activity most businesses remained, by modern standards tiny. Glyn's, one of the larger banks, had only thirty-six staff in 1815. The Bank of England with almost a thousand clerks was huge and unrivalled.

150. Guy's Hospital in south London, founded by Thomas Guy on the proceeds of his South Sea gamble.

151. The hub of London's commercial life – the Bank of England. A perspective view of 1743. The building was designed by George Sampson.

TRADE AND EXPANSION

Despite the trauma of the 'Bubble', and against a background of continuing wars against France and Spain, the Georgian City prospered mightily. Nelson himself put the crux of the matter most pithily: "The City of London ... exists by victories at sea." Naval power underpinned the growth of a formal and informal empire which enabled Britain and, above all, London to meet the needs of constantly expanding markets by importing and often re-exporting tropical and semi-tropical products such as tea, coffee, sugar, tobacco, rice, indigo and mahogany and raw materials, such as timber, wool, hemp, leather, tallow and grain. The processing of these goods created employment in the sprawling slums east and south of the City, where beer was brewed, sugar was boiled and fine woods turned into elegant furniture.

Commerce and finance were still deeply intertwined. Barclays Bank can be traced back to a linen-drapers. Dealing in basic commodities, and insuring against their loss or damage at sea, drove the life of the City itself. Servicing the finances of a government and

152. (Below) Hoare's Bank in Fleet Street. Founded c.1672, the bank moved to its present site in Fleet Street in 1690. Customers included Pepys, Dryden and Evelyn.

153. (Right) Child's Bank next to the Temple Bar in Fleet Street.

154. *Capel's new offices in Throgmorton Street in 1854.*

empire which was constantly expanding the scale of its operations provided another valuable stimulus, although even the Bank of England still regarded itself as a private business, rather than as an arm of the state. Institutionalisation proceeded piecemeal, nevertheless. *Lloyd's List* was first published in 1734. The year 1773 witnessed two significant developments – the formation of a bankers' clearing house system and the formal establishment of the Stock Exchange.

The most obvious signs of the Georgian City's prosperity were the handsome Mansion House built as the official residence of the Lord Mayor, Dance's eccentric new facade for Guildhall, Sir John Soane's mighty rebuilding of the Bank of England and such elegant new churches as All Hallows under the Wall and St Botolph's, Aldgate. As the City literally swelled even its ancient gates were demolished in 1760-1.

The long rivalry with France culminated in the titanic struggle from 1792 to 1815, which decisively confirmed the City's hegemony over both international trade and the emerging world of international finance. Amsterdam, occupied by the French in 1795, was finally extinguished as a significant rival. As Napoleon's empire spread over Europe, capital fled to London as the only safe haven and so did capitalists. The disruption to business in Hamburg and Frankfurt brought Britain the Schroders, the Brandts and the Rothschilds. They joined a commercial community in which Huguenots and Jews – Cazenoves and Bosanquets, Mocattas and Goldsmids – were already prominent. The nineteenth century would see the further arrival of Kleinworts from Germany and Hambros from Denmark. This cosmopolitanism was counter-balanced by a constant infusion of native talent from the provinces. The Quaker Gurneys hailed from Norfolk, James Capel from Worcester and Brown, Shipley grew out of the Liverpool trade.

The continued expansion of the City's overseas trade threatened to choke the Pool of London. Visitors might wonder at the teeming forest of masts and gawp at the Cockney boast that it was possible to cross from bank to bank across the decks of close-packed ships but congestion led to gross inefficiency as vessels waited, usually a week, often a month, to gain access to a berth. Immobility increased vulnerability to pilferage. City interests resisted remedial innovations, partly out of unthinking conservatism, partly out of a fear that their business might disappear downstream. Salvation came in the shape of a River Police force (1798) and the West India Docks, cut through the Isle of Dogs (1802) and linked to the City by the aptly-named Commercial Road in 1803. Surrey Commercial Docks on the south side of the river followed in 1807 and St Katharine's, in the shadow of the Tower, in 1828. The 'Royals' further downstream opened between 1855 and 1880 but even with their hydraulic cranes and railways could scarcely keep pace with the ever-rising volume of commodities passing through the capital. A Royal Commission reported in 1902 that the Port of London was ill-equipped, inefficient, expensive and ill-managed by a plethora of conflicting boards and bodies. To remedy the situation a streamlined Port of London Authority came into being in 1909, combining representatives from the Board of Trade, Admiralty, Trinity House, L.C.C. and City Corporation.

UNCERTAINTY AND INTELLECT

Industrialisation gradually broadened the scope of the stock market from solely dealing in government securities to embrace shares in canals, docks, gas and water companies, mines and, most significantly, railways. As both government and public slowly assimilated the free-market doctrines of Adam Smith, the East India Company finally lost its trading monopoly in Asia and the Bank of England assumed a more overtly central role as the monopoly supplier of currency notes.

The City was becoming a more sophisticated place but scarcely more secure.

Every decade had its major panic – over Latin America in the 1820s, the United States in the 1830s, 'railway mania' in the 1840s, the US again in the 1850s and the collapse of the great bill-broking house of Overend, Gurney and Co. in the 1860s. These episodes underlined the City's 'image problem'. The radical journalist William Cobbett, who railed most violently against the 'Great Wen' in general as the nation's bloodsucker, was even more violent when it came to the City in particular – a viper's nest of parasites, Jews and other foreigners, spewing forth paper money. Even the slightly gentler 'country critique' vilified the City as a gross monster, corrupt and privileged, presided over by gross Aldermen, venial and duplicitous, whose sole cultural interests were the pleasures of the table.

This was going too far. City life involved, if it did not exactly attract, at least a few figures of outstanding intellect. Two of the most eminent philosophers of the age, James Mill (1773-1836) and his son John Stuart Mill (1806-73) served successively as heads of the office of the East India Company. David Ricardo (1772-1823), the London-born son of a Dutch Jew, was not only the founder of classical economics but also an active and successful stockbroker. George Grote (1794-1871) was a banker, albeit a very reluctant one, before retiring to write a definitive eight-volume history of ancient Greece and become Vice-Chancellor of the University of London. Another banker in a family firm, George Goschen (1831-1907) wrote an influential work on the 'Theory of the Foreign Exchanges' (1861) as well as becoming Chancellor of the Exchequer (1886-92) and playing a crucial role in

155. *New office buildings and warehouses in London became increasingly ornate from the mid-19th century. This bizarre building, a warehouse, in Eastcheap was designed by R.L. Roumieu. The building still survives.*

156. John Stuart Mill.

stabilising the Baring crisis which rocked the City in 1890. Walter Bagehot (1826-77) worked in his father's shipowning and banking business before becoming editor of *The Economist* and writing that classic critique of City operations *Lombard Street* (1873).   In fairness, however, it must also be admitted that some of the City's most vehement cultural critics – designer-craftsman William Morris (1834-96) and art-historian John Ruskin (1819-1900) – were both sons of City businessmen. Both Morris and Ruskin were quintessential Oxford men and a university education remained very much the exception rather than the rule in the City.

Although trade, rather than finance, remained the dominant business of the City, finance was fast becoming its rival, for reasons the *Quarterly Review* explained in 1872:

Political distrust and revolution in France, the absence of unity and coherence between North and South Germany ... combine with the unquestioned stability and credit of English institutions, the benefit of firm and equal laws, and the facilities and inducements of the freest ports, the lowest tariff, and the cheapest manufactures in the world, to render London the place of ultimate settlement of the largest part of the business of both hemispheres. Hence the accumulation here of foreign capital and the growth of a powerful class of banks and financial houses..."

By 1897 Nathan Rothschild could state that Britain was "in general the Bank for the whole world" – and for Britain, read London, for London, read the City.

The global reach of City operations was symbolized by the presence of dozens of foreign institutions. The Ottoman Bank arrived in 1863, Credit Lyonnais in 1870, Chase Manhattan in 1887 and the Bank of Japan in 1898.

157. The City Terminus Hotel at Cannon Street station, designed by E.M. Barry and opened in May 1867.   Despite its size, there were only 84 bedrooms since much of the space was taken up by public rooms. It was used extensively for public and company meetings. Ironically, in the very heart of British capitalism, the Communist Party of Great Britain was founded here in 1920.

FROM RESIDENTS TO COMMUTERS

As the City refined its character as a working community, so it redefined its character as a residential community. In 1815 it still had not only thousands of craftsmen living above the shop where they made and sold gloves, breeches or clocks but even small factories making such homely products as wallpaper and mattresses. With a residential population of 122,000 the City was still the most densely-populated part of the metropolis but that figure now represented only ten per cent of the total.

By 1845 the financial journalist David Morier Evans could observe that:

The City is not now much chosen for a residence. The old houses, in the best thoroughfares, are either let as offices, or given up to the occupation of housekeepers ... At the banks, the rule is, for the junior partner to reside on the premises; and a certain number of clerks, also, live in the house.

By 1851 there were still 129,000 people living in the City and they still included hundreds of tailors, bootmakers and other artisans. Cheapside still rivalled the West End as a retailing area. But there were now few resident bankers or merchants. The richest preferred apartments in Regent Street or Regent's Park. The second rank took villas in Kensington or Blackheath or even further afield. William Morris's father commuted by stage-coach from Walthamstow, then a rural retreat on the edge of Epping Forest. This was relative luxury; more typical were the two hundred thousand people who walked or took an omnibus into the City daily from areas such as Islington, Hackney, Peckham and Clapham.

The turning-point came in the 1860s with the construction of major new railway termini which made commuting practicable for the masses. Fenchurch Street dated back to 1841 but until 1849 locomotives on that line had stopped at Blackwall, leaving coaches to be hauled to the Minories by cable. A new station was opened in 1854. The other eastern terminus remained at Shoreditch until Liverpool Street, the last and largest of the City termini, opened in 1874. It was commuters from other directions who benefited most from the new stations of the 1860s. Farringdon, opened in 1864, enabled travellers from the Thames Valley to complete their journey from Paddington by the new Underground. Broad Street, opened in 1865, was originally intended for freight, to link the Midlands to London's docks, but by 1900 it had become the City's third busiest passenger station. Ludgate Hill, also opened in 1865, served as the hub for a network of suburban services stretching out as far as Enfield, Richmond and Crystal Palace. Cannon Street, opened in 1866, boasted E.M. Barry's imposing City Terminus Hotel, the setting for many important company meetings and, ironically, the foundation of the Communist Party of Great Britain in 1920. Holborn Viaduct, opened in 1874, also had a station hotel.

158. *New offices in Throgmorton Street, 1870.*

By 1871 the resident population of the City had begun to fall in absolute as well as relative terms to 75,000. By 1901 it was just 27,000. The small traders and retailers had now followed the financiers of previous generations out to the suburbs.

Changes in the City's population were reflected in changes in its appearance. The destruction by fire of the second Royal Exchange in 1838 necessitated reconstruction of one of its most prominent landmarks. Specialised markets like the Baltic Exchange and Coal Exchange acquired fine new premises. Spurred on, perhaps, by the achievements of the Metropolitan Board of Works elsewhere in the capital, the City Corporation sponsored major improvements within its own boundaries, largely under the direction of City Surveyor, Sir Horace Jones (1819-97). Eastcheap was widened; Queen Victoria Street was laid out to link Blackfriars bridge with Bank junction; Wren's Temple Bar – "the bone in the throat of Fleet Street"

159. Holborn Viaduct, one of the major improvement works in the City of London. This is a sectional drawing showing the position of supply pipes. Also included in the bottom centre, is the Pneumatic Dispatch Railway.

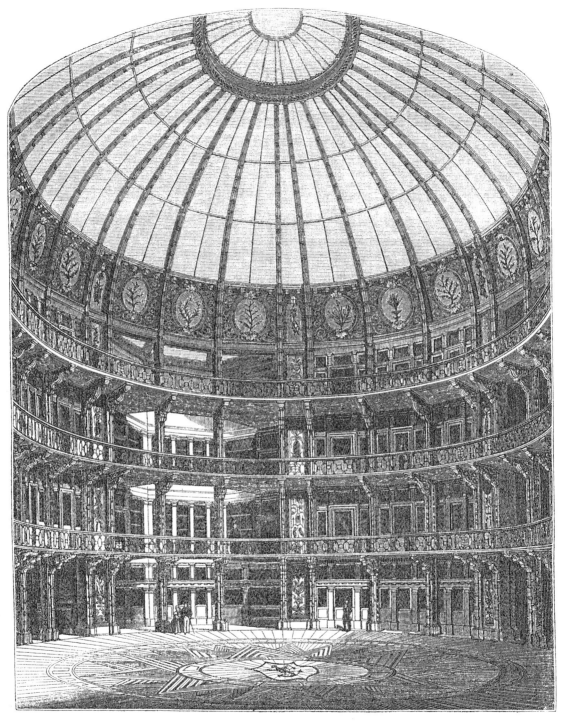

160. *The interior of the magnificent new Coal Exchange on Lower Thames Street, designed by James Bunning. This building was demolished by the City Corporation with unseemly haste, against many protests, in the 1960s.*

Temple Bar – "the bone in the throat of Fleet Street" – was demolished and replaced by a flamboyant column surmounted by an heraldic dragon to mark the western boundary of the 'Square Mile'. Ornate new market buildings were erected at Smithfield, Leadenhall and Billingsgate. At Holborn the valley of the river Fleet was bridged by the construction of the Holborn Viaduct. In 1878 Epping Forest was acquired as a conservation area and Highgate Woods were subsequently purchased for the further refreshment of Londoners and to the eternal frustration of speculative developers. (Hampstead Heath, which the City also manages, was acquired when the Greater London Council was abolished in 1986.)

Among private businesses, insurance companies, the Atlas, Alliance, Sun, Globe and Imperial, led the way in building Italianate palazzi. The banks were next to follow, with the National Provincial in Bishopsgate an outstanding example. At the same time centuries-old landmarks, like the East India House and the legendary Garraway's coffee-house, were vanishing. Of all City buildings existing in 1855, four-fifths had been rebuilt by 1905. Almost invariably this involved raising their height, overshadowing Wren's steeples and increasing the City's available floor-space by 50%. Gas-lighting pierced the gloom between the new office canyons.

These buildings were populated by new breeds of worker. In 1851 there were 16,420 clerks in London; by 1891 five times as many, the first generation to be produced by an elementary education system compulsory for all. The new technologies of typewriter and telephone almost immediately became female preserves, increasing the number of female clerical staff from a mere 7,000 in 1881 to 146,000 by 1911. In both cases the largest concentrations of these vastly expanded numbers were to be found in the City proper.

From 1891 onwards the new armies of office-workers could travel into Bank by a new means of transport, the true 'Underground'. The early lines, the District, Circle and Metropolitan, ran just beneath the surface of the streets, their stations open to the sky for fumes and vapours to disperse, their platforms reachable by a flight or two of steps. When the first section of what is now the Northern line (then the City and South London) opened, it did so as a true 'Tube', running in a tunnel deep beneath the earth and propelled by electric traction.

161. The prevailing Italianate gothic style of architecture is shown in this building – a warehouse – in Upper Thames Street, depicted in The Builder *in 1866.*

The Years Between

BUSINESS AS USUAL

After the armistice of 1918 war memorials at High Holborn and outside the Royal Exchange commemorated the tens of thousands of City workers who would never return, but the City, like Britain as a whole, appeared to have shrugged off the trauma of war in its desire to return to business as usual. The City had been bombed for the first time in its history, but the physical damage inflicted had been slight. One bomb, falling at West Smithfield, had stripped away the plastering on the chambers above the archway into St Bartholomew-the-Great and revealed its half-timbering. More profoundly, financing the hostilities had required Britain to sell off much of its portfolio of overseas holdings, largely to the benefit of the United States. The centrality and supremacy of the City and the pound sterling in the global system of trading and finance would henceforth come under increasing challenge from New York.

In the daily life of the City there was no transformation comparable to the great changes of the late Victorian period, but rather a continuation of those trends. This contrasted strongly with the dramatic developments on London's fringes, with its new world of

arterial roads and electrically-powered, smokeless factories and speculatively-built estates of semi-detached houses. Whereas London's population overall continued to rise to reach its all-time peak in 1939, by 1931 the residential population of the City had fallen to 11,000. The Pool of London, however, remained a working port, with warehouses and cranes lining its southern edge. Much of its labour force still lived within walking distance to the east and the south, often in conditions of mid-Victorian squalor.

TRAFFIC AND TRANSPORT

Traffic problems in the Square Mile were as bad as ever but took a slightly different form. Motor taxis had largely replaced horse-drawn cabs even before 1914 and in the 1920s motor buses began to add to the City's traditional congestion, as pirate buses competed, often recklessly, with their rivals of the General Omnibus Company for fares. The extension of the Underground system north-westwards into Metroland meant that City workers could commute from leafy avenues of villas as far away as Harrow or even Aylesbury. Longer commuting times offset the gains in leisure time yielded by a trend towards a shorter working-day. For the poorer clerks, who needed to take advantage of cheap early-morning workmen's fares, a later starting-time actually made the morning journey both a nightmare and a non-

162. Traffic congestion in London was not a new problem. This scene, outside the Mansion House, was drawn about 1859.

163. *As Gustave Doré saw traffic congestion in London; the scene is Ludgate Hill.*

sense, as a 1930s commuter from Eltham remembered:

> When you got to the station it was like a football match, absolutely solid packed with people. To get a workman's ticket, you see, you had to arrive in central London by eight o'clock, so you had to catch the 7.36 train. Everyone wanted to catch it. Because a lot of us on those new estates didn't have any money to spare (we were all paying for our houses) you'd even find people who didn't start work till nine or ten o'clock, clerical-type people, they would all catch that last workman's train as well to get the cheap fare. And even when it arrived, it was practically full up with people ... so we'd be waiting on the platform four or five lines deep ... It was really unpleasant, everybody would be shoving, pushing, there would be shouting, elbowing, near fighting sometimes ... Sometimes you couldn't get on, but even when you did, you'd stand all the way, about twenty of you in a compartment meant for eight.

The creation of the London Passenger Transport Board in 1933 established an overall body with coordinating powers which could begin to impose some order on the chaos of the capital's transport systems but the only major initiative taken by the City itself in the inter-war period was the reconstruction of Southwark Bridge in 1921.

THE LOOK OF THINGS

In the City's streets electricity began to replace gas lighting and in its offices American-made adding-machines and duplicators joined the telephone and typewriter in raising clerical productivity. The proportion of female clerical workers continued to increase but most employers still expected them to resign their positions on marriage.

The Edwardian look of the City was confirmed by the continuing preference of corporations for 'Banker's Baroque'. Business could command the services of the most senior members of the architectural profession and did so. Sir Edwin Cooper's imposing Port of London Authority building at Trinity Square, begun in 1912, was completed in 1922. The same architect was also responsible for a new Lloyd's building and Royal Mail House in Leadenhall Street, a new Banque Belge in Bishopsgate and a massive headquarters building for the National Westminster Bank at the corner of Poultry and Princes' Street. Next door to it stood Sir Edwin Lutyens' Midland Bank headquarters. Lutyens' other City projects included Britannic House for British Petroleum in Finsbury Circus, offices for the Hudson's Bay Company at 52 Bishopsgate, a Midland Bank branch building in Leadenhall Street, near it, in the same thoroughfare, the Cunard building and in Fleet Street a new headquarters for Reuter's and the Press Association. Sir John Burnet's most prominent work was Adelaide House, with its distinctive Egyptian cornice, overshadowing Wren's church of St Magnus the Martyr at the northern end of London Bridge. He also built the Lloyds Bank building on Cornhill and Lombard Street where T.S. Eliot came to work and Unilever House at Blackfriars, where de Keyser's Hotel once stood. Arthur J. Davis, surviving partner of Mewes and Davis, architects of the pre-war Ritz in Piccadilly, built for the National Westminster Bank at 9 Old Broad Street and 51-2 Threadneedle Street and for Morgan Grenfell at 23 Great Winchester Street. Sir Aston Webb, who had re-fronted Buckingham Palace, designed office-buildings at 24 Bishopsgate and 36-44 Moorgate. Most of these edifices were variations on a theme by Wren. As Professor Pevsner has observed, with evident impatience, it was not until the 1950s that buildings in a truly twentieth century idiom began to appear in the City. The only striking exception to this generalisation was Sir Owen

164. The Port of London Authority building in Trinity Square, built between 1912 and 1922 to the designs of Sir Edwin Cooper.

165. Construction of the Unilever building on the Embankment, on the site of the De Keyser Hotel.

Williams' *Daily Express* building in Fleet Street with its uncompromising, (or flashy, depending on your taste) black glass and chromium facade.

The largest single construction project was the re-building of Sir John Soane's Bank of England, which dominates the City's very centre. Soane's one-storey masterpiece had become hopelessly over-crowded. Given its confinement on an island site, the only way to build was up. Sir Herbert Baker, collaborator with Lutyens on the building of New Delhi, was licensed to tear the heart out of Soane's work. Pevsner summarised the outcome as "the worst individual loss suffered by London architecture in the first half of the twentieth century" but conceded that, economically speaking, there was probably no alternative.

The emergence of wireless broadcasting in the 1920s constituted little challenge to the continuing supremacy of Fleet Street. Until the end of the decade the BBC obligingly declined to issue news bulletins before six pm lest newspaper sales be damaged and on one celebrated occasion even announced that "there is no news today." The *Daily Telegraph* and *Daily Express* both rebuilt their offices and Reuter's moved into its new headquarters just opposite them. Northcliffe having died, the presiding genius of Fleet Street was the buccaneering Canadian, Max Aitken (1879-1964). A son of the manse, he was already a millionaire by the time he emigrated to Britain in his early thirties. A compulsive intriguer in business and politics, he made the *Daily Express* the most widely-read daily in the world and established the *Sunday Express* and *Evening Standard* as its stable-mates. His dynamism and administrative drive brought him the post of minister of information in the first world war and minister of aircraft production in the second as well as ennoblement as Baron Beaverbrook of Beaverbrook and Cherkley. H.G. Wells opined that if "the Beaver" ever got to Heaven he would be "chucked out for trying to pull off a merger between Heaven and Hell ... after having secured a controlling interest in key subsidiary companies in both places, of course."

A Devastated City

UNPREPARED

"The flying peril is not a peril from which one can fly.... We cannot move London," Churchill warned the House of Commons five years before the outbreak of the Second World War. The major objective of the Luftwaffe was less to pulverize London as such than to bring its life, and especially that of its port, to a standstill. In neither did it succeed, but the damage it inflicted was indeed grievous.

For Londoners the Blitz began with a late afternoon raid on the docks and East End on 7 September 1940. It killed 430, wounded over 1,600 and cruelly revealed the ill-prepared state of the capital's emergency services. Four-fifths of the twenty-thousand hastily-recruited men of the Auxiliary Fire Service had never fought a real blaze before. In anticipation of daylight visitations dropping poison gas, the authorities had distributed millions of gas-masks. What they had to deal with was night raiders dropping high explosives and incendiaries. What they needed were shelters and searchlights, barrage-balloons and anti-aircraft batteries to interdict low-level precision bombing and 'Heavy Rescue' squads with mobile cranes to extricate victims from collapsed buildings. All this took time to learn and more time to organise.

On 12 September raiders dropped a land-mine which lodged itself beneath the south-west tower of St Paul's Cathedral. It took three days to extricate, a feat which won the two demolition engineers the George Cross, and, when detonated on Hackney Marshes, made a crater a hundred yards across.

THE SECOND GREAT FIRE

The worst raid on the City proper came on Sunday 29 December 1940, the one hundred and fourteenth night of the Blitz and three weeks after the last heavy raid on the City itself. As it was the last Sunday of the old year, the City was even more than usually deserted, as many residents had gone to stay with relatives to see in the New Year. As it was a weekend, business premises were securely locked.

Thick cloud cover seemed to make it unlikely that the Luftwaffe would attempt anything more than a 'normal' nuisance raid. But the Luftwaffe was preparing something special, based on its success in burning out the heart of Manchester a week previously. The plan was to send in two waves, the first of which, some 140 strong, would be loaded almost entirely with incendiaries, while the second, slightly larger, loaded with high explosive, would deliver the knockout blow on an already blazing and clearly visible

target. The date chosen for the raid coincided – not accidentally – with an especially low tide for the Thames, so that fire-boats, marooned in a narrow mid-channel would be out of range of riverside flames.

The City was no longer the wooden tinderbox that had been ravaged by walls of flame in 1666. But the grim brick and stone facades of its office buildings and warehouses were deceptive. Within, most were packed with combustibles – floors, doors, desks, shelving, stairways, packing crates, stationery, textiles, printers' inks, fuel for heating systems, a warehouse full of 'Brasso' metal polish and, in the offices of twenty-seven publishing firms around St Paul's Churchyard, five million books. There were also numerous targets of direct military significance – the bridges over the Thames, three major telephone exchanges and half a dozen railway stations – plus dozens of historic buildings of great symbolic value to the morale of a beleaguered city, above all, St Paul's.

Led by veteran pathfinders, the first wave of bombers hit the City at just after 6.00 pm. Within an hour a hundred fires had been reported and the City's primary water main had been fractured by a direct hit from a 550 pound high explosive bomb. Many of the crews of the two thousand appliances brought into action would only be able to stand by helplessly as their hoses ran dry. At Guildhall fire-watchers successfully extinguished every fire that started, until sparks from the burning spire of St Lawrence Jewry – locked and inaccessible to fire-fighters – set fire to the roof and forced them to salvage its historic documents and treasures and abandon the building to its fate.

At the Cathedral the dedicated 'St Paul's Watch' team of staff and volunteers had greater success. The immense dome, weighing 64,000 tons, was built of wood, covered only by a protective skin of lead, easily penetrated by a cigar-shaped bomb dropped from thousands of feet above. At 6.39 Cannon Street fire station received a call reporting that the cathedral's dome was on fire, with an incendiary lodged in a joint between two timbers. Before they could respond, it had been dealt with. Later another one lodged halfway through the lead skin until it burned itself free and fell under its own weight to where it could be smothered safely. Meanwhile buildings blazed all around - only yards away on the northern side, where the stocks of the publishers of St Paul's Churchyard and Paternoster Row raged out of control.

Without radio communications the firefighters were completely dependent on telephones to sustain their command and control system. As lines were severed and two of the three main exchanges hit, this system disintegrated. The City's five fire stations were themselves threatened. Redcross Street station had to be evacuated. But it was hours before the sheer scale of

166. *The bombed devastation north of St Paul's.*

the disaster was clearly understood and reserve brigades summoned in from Kent, Essex and Surrey. Nor was the fire-storm, raging at 4,000 degrees Fahrenheit, confined to the City alone. An entire swathe of warehouses along the south side of the Thames, from London Bridge to Tower Bridge, was alight, threatening Waterloo, London Bridge station and Guy's Hospital. To the north Old Street, lined with empty premises, was ablaze and the close-packed streets of Islington were pock-marked with burning houses and tenements. The night sky was lit so intensely that the glow was seen at Bishop's Stortford, almost thirty miles away towards Cambridge.

It was 7.30 am, over thirteen hours after the raid began, before the fires were contained and it took a further three days damping down to extinguish them completely. Although bombs had fallen as far south as Croydon and as far north as Hampstead, most of the 24,000 incendiaries dropped over the course of six hours had been squarely on target, starting over a thousand separate fires. In the east, the Tower had been spared major damage, but Fenchurch Street station was out of action, although not for long, and the areas immediately east and west of it were gutted, as were the blocks between Houndsditch and Middlesex Street and either side of Cannon Street. The worst devastation was in the west. The area bounded by Moorgate on the east, Aldersgate Street on the west, the Artillery Ground on the north and Gresham Street on the south was simply burned out, as were the streets around St Paul's, except for a patch to its south-west, and off Fleet Street, especially on the northern side. Five Thames bridges were blocked. The telephone exchanges at Wood Street and King Edward Street had both been put out of action. Of the City stations, only Liverpool Street remained operational.

Guildhall's sturdy walls still stood but within lay a chaos of smouldering timbers. Apart from St Lawrence Jewry, twelve other Wren churches, including St Bride's, St Giles, Cripplegate and Christchurch, Greyfriars, had either been completely gutted or severely damaged, as had All Hallows by the Tower and three other survivors of 1666. Only eight of these seventeen would subsequently be rebuilt. Whole streets – Redcross Street, Jewin Street, Dowgate Dock – would vanish from the map for ever. Twelve firemen had been killed and over two hundred and fifty injured. Civilian casualties amounted to a hundred and fifty dead and five hundred injured, the majority being outside the City itself, especially in Islington.

Amazingly, the District line had kept running for hours after the raid started and, sheltered in the basement of their sturdy building on Queen Victoria Street, the printers of *The Times* had ensured that it appeared as usual.

And much had survived. The Mansion House, Bank and Royal Exchange were unscathed. The top floor of Dr Johnson's house in Gough Square, where he had composed his famous *Dictionary*, had caught fire but the damage had been contained. Above all, literally and metaphorically, St Paul's still stood, a majestic reassurance to bemused workers picking their way through the sodden debris to find out if they had anywhere left to work. And it could have been so much worse. Thanks to rain, the second wave of Luftwaffe bombers, carrying high-explosive, had been unable to take off.

....AND AFTER

The City's trauma provoked a national debate, as a result of which a mandatory system of fire-watching was introduced and an integrated national fire service set up.

December 29th was the worst raid, but by no means the last. A fortnight later, on 11 January 1941, a direct hit on Bank Underground station killed over a hundred shelterers. There were further heavy raids on 8 March, 19 March, 16 April and 19 April. The last major raid occurred on 10 May 1941, a clear night with a 'bomber's moon' and so unseasonably cold that it was literally freezing. Five hundred planes dropped seven hundred tons of high explosive right across the capital, plus enough incendiaries to start two thousand fires. Fire brigades from as far away as the Midlands and the West Country were called in but nine fires were still out of control the following morning. The House of Commons, Royal Courts of Justice and Tower of London were all hit, 1,436 people were killed, 12,000 made homeless and 155,000 families were cut off from gas or electricity. The night-fighters of the RAF, so ineffectual the previous autumn, were now hitting back with effect but, even so, had raids on such a scale continued it is difficult to imagine that port and City could have gone on functioning effectively. But the onslaught ceased as suddenly as it had begun as German efforts were switched to the invasion of Russia. For three years there would be no serious attacks. Then came the flying bombs. For the City the worst incident was at Smithfield, in March 1945, when a V2 rocket killed 380 people.

Post-war City

A SIXTIES PERSPECTIVE

'Post-war City' may seem a slightly flat title for a concluding chapter but it does point up the overwhelming fact that shaped the City's development for a quarter of a century – the sheer need for physical reconstruction after the destruction wrought by the Blitz. From the perspective of the 1960s this did not seem to have been happily accomplished. There had been a few undoubted gains. The construction of Bucklersbury House on Queen Victoria Street revealed the long-lost Temple of Mithras. The Mermaid opened as the City's first theatre since Puritan times. Many Wren churches had been restored, if not always to their former glory; likewise Guildhall and Middle Temple Hall. St Paul's now boasted an American Memorial Chapel and a flamboyant baroque high altar and pulpit. Sir Albert Richardson's nearby *Financial Times* building was to be the first postwar City building to achieve listed status but the Bank of England extension over the way from it, in New Change, was to draw forth Professor Pevsner's full venom – "it is almost beyond comprehension how a design that would have been reactionary twenty years before could have been put into execution in the 1950s." Architect Michael Floyd, writing in Ian

Norrie's 1961 compilation, *The Book of the City*, was bitter in his summary of the general quality of the rebuilt cityscape – "the destruction of so many City buildings during the war was an architectural disaster; the rebuilding that has taken place since has been a greater one." In 1962 came the demolition of the 1849 Coal Exchange, a pioneering example of the structural use of cast-iron, its extinction widely condemned as an unforgivable act of senseless vandalism. By the mid-1960s architectural critic Ian Nairn sensed that the distinctive character of the City was being leached out of it by " ... the false idea that the upper crust of the City has of itself. Clean the buildings, bleach the Wren woodwork, pile on the civic banquets, but for God's sake don't actually *live* there." Demolition continued alongside reconstruction, taking with it such landmarks as Cockerell's 1842 Sun Life Assurance building in Threadneedle Street, the Stock Exchange of 1853 and Cannon Street Station Hotel. Broad Street station declined and decayed.

UPWARD, OUTWARD .... AND ONWARD?

The 1970s saw the unmistakable acceptance of the skyscraper, most notably in the form of a new home for the Stock Exchange and a towering headquarters building for the National Westminster Bank, at six hundred feet high still the tallest in the Square Mile. A new split-level Museum of London was opened; its design won prizes from experts but not from tourists,

167. The Mermaid Theatre in 1995.

168. *The NatWest Tower, designed by Richard Seifert, in Broad Street, 1995.*

169. *The Lloyd's building, designed by Richard Rogers, in 1995.*

confused about how one could actually get into it.

The early 1980s witnessed the completion of the ambitious Barbican arts complex, whose residential towers were supposed to bring genuine residents back into the City but in many cases were simply used as convenient accommodation for short-stay visitors or high-profile metropolitans who week-ended elsewhere.

Louise Nicholson's modestly-titled *Definitive Guide to London* summarised the achievement with a grudging measure of approbation:

Looking on the good side, it has three virtues. First, it was the only dream that became reality for the great post-war developers who wanted to turn London into a vast and desolate high-rise, high-walkway nightmare ... Second, war damage here was so bad that few buildings were demolished to make way for it. Third, if you can find your way into this maze, the residential blocks are grouped around a restored St Giles, Cripplegate, a huge stretch of Roman wall and defences, and a fine arts complex ...

What might have marked the end of a great phase of rebuilding in fact marked the beginning of an even greater one, comparable to the reconstruction which followed the Great Fire or gutted Dickens' London in the 1860s and 1870s. The impact of new electronic technology and management styles rendered the office-blocks of the 1960s and 1970s obsolete, both technically and culturally. Over little more than a

decade almost half the City's building stock was replaced – but with a net gain of only about 12% in floor-space. The main customer was the financial services sector; insurance companies decanted to cheaper locations, in many cases outside the capital altogether, vacating 3,600,000 square feet over the course of a decade.

The decline of retailing in the City received overdue attention. Marks & Spencer opened two substantial new stores. Japanese and Korean restaurants became commonplace. Wine bars, although by no means a novelty, seemed to become almost as numerous as the traditional pub. The removal of the railway bridge across Ludgate Hill opened up a splendid frontal vista towards St Paul's. Billingsgate was vacated and renovated – but remained untenanted.

The collapse of the Thatcherite property boom after 1987 scarcely checked the pace of change, as so many projects were already in the pipeline. The boom stretched out to fringe areas like London Bridge, Aldgate and Finsbury. In 1984 when the surge was just getting under way 2,100,000 square feet were completed – in 1991 7,100,000. Bigger was accompanied by better, with a greater emphasis on quality in building or at least quality in external finishing. Pink granite became something of a cliche as a cladding for steel-framed buildings. A jungle-filled atrium be-

170. Alban Gate in London Wall.

171. 'Commuters', a sculpture decorating the new Broadgate development in the City, 1995.

came *de rigeur*. Richard Rogers' controversial 1986 Lloyd's building was matched by the neo-Gothic pastiche of the 1992 Minster Court. Liverpool Street station was handsomely refurbished. Next door to it the Broadgate Centre, on the site of Broad Street station, brought City workers the lunch-time delight of ice-skating and an intriguing collection of outdoor sculptures. On Ludgate Hill the City acquired its first station in a century, City Thameslink. At Cannon Street station an entire office-block was in effect inserted above the platforms, between the Victorian twin brick towers. Three massive blocks were shoehorned into Fleet Place and another two along the lower end of New Bridge Street. At London Wall Terry Farrell's post-modern Alban Gate loomed right over the roadway. The exuberant gilded banking-hall of the old National Provincial Building in Bishopsgate was restored to its former splendour, if not its former use.

Such gains were offset by the 1993 IRA bombing of Bishopsgate, which did £800,000,000 worth of damage and reduced ancient St Ethelburga's, a survivor of both the Great Fire and the Blitz, to a pile of rubble. A year later the Templeton Report called for the City's twenty-two active churches to be reduced to four. Although the physical survival of the rest was guaranteed, finding an appropriate use for them and funding their maintenance remained an unsolved problem on the agenda. Turning them over to Livery Companies who did not have their own Halls seemed at least a possibility in keeping with the traditions of the City. *Pace* the restless spirits of Ian Nairn and Professor Pevsner, the fact that an exhibition of plans for the future of Paternoster Square had to be extended on account of the public interest it generated does suggest that the future *may* remedy some of the errors of the recent past, rather than compound them.

Further Reading

C. Amery: *Wren's London* (1988)

Caroline Barron: The Medieval Guildhall of London (1974)

S. Barson and A. Saint: *A Farewell to Fleet Street* (1988)

G.W. Bell: *The Great Fire of London* (1920)

Robert J. Blackham: *London For Ever : The Sovereign City* (n.d.)

Mary Cathcart Borer: *The City of London : A History* (1977)

Ray Boston: *Fleet Street : Its History and Influence* (1990)

Susan Brigden: London and the Reformation (1989)

C. Brooke and G. Keir: *London 800-1216 : The Shaping of a City* (1975)

Corporation of the City of London: *The City of London : A Record of Destruction and Survival* (1951)

T. Dyson: *The Medieval London Waterfront* (1989)

I. Grant and N. Maddren: *The City at War* (1975)

Jenny Hall and Ralph Merrifield: *Roman London* (1986)

D. Johnson: *The City Ablaze : the second great fire of London 29 December 1940* (1980)

David Kynaston: *The City of London : A World of Its Own 1815-1890* (1994)

D. Lloyd (ed.): *Save the City : a conservation study of the City of London* (1976)

Hamish Macrae and Frances Cairncross: *Capital City : London as a Financial Centre* (Revised ed.1984)

Peter Marsden: Roman London (1980)

Marin Mason and Malcolm Sanders: *The City Companion* (1994)

R. Merrifield: *London – City of the Romans* (1983)

R. Michie: *The City of London : Continuity and Change 1850-1990* (1992)

G. Milne: *The Great Fire of London* (1986)

Belinda Morse: *Square Mile Walks : Six Walks in the City of London* (1989)

Ian Norrie (ed.): *The Book of the City* (1961)

Charles Pendrill: Old Parish Life in London (1937)

Nikolaus Pevsner: *The Buildings of England, London Vol. One : The Cities of London and Westminster* (Revised ed. 1973)

T.F. Reddaway: *The Rebuilding of London after the Great Fire* (1940)

John Schofield: *The Building of London from the Conquest to the Great Fire* (1984)

S.L. Thrupp: *The Merchant Class of Medieval London* (1948)

A. Vince: *Saxon London : An Archaeological Investigation* (1990)

Ben Weinreb and Christopher Hibbert: *The London Encyclopedia* (1983)

Gwyn A. Williams: Medieval London from Commune to Capital (1963)

INDEX

Illustrations are denoted by an asterisk